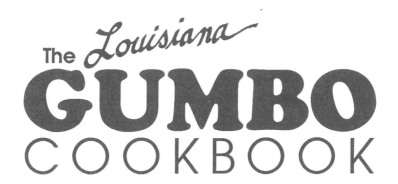

The *Louisiana* GUMBO COOKBOOK

BEA & FLOYD WEBER

Acadian House
PUBLISHING
LAFAYETTE, LOUISIANA

ABOUT THE COVER: Seafood Gumbo is a south Louisiana delicacy that can be found in homes and restaurants in New Orleans and throughout the Cajun country. This one was prepared at Don's Seafood Hut in Lafayette. The recipe can be found on page 114.

ISBN: 0-925417-13-0

♦ Published by Acadian House Publishing, Lafayette, Louisiana

♦ Graphic design and illustrations by Tom Sommers, Crowley, Louisiana

♦ Cover photography by John Daigre, New Iberia, Louisiana

♦ Color separation by Orleans Colour, New Orleans, Louisiana

♦ Printed by Walsworth Press, Marceline, Missouri

Foreword

Compiling recipes and background information for a book like this required some of the same virtues that are needed to make a good gumbo: a degree of culinary skill, a good measure of patience, and a generous amount of tender loving care.

Bea and Floyd Weber went through nearly 1,000 gumbo recipes before settling on the 115 or so that make up the body of this book. Work on the project began in 1989 and went on, full-time, for two solid years.

Floyd researched and compiled the history of gumbo, sought out and secured permission from the various authors and publishers to use their recipes, and generally worked as the keeper of the files and records. Bea set up a test kitchen in their home and proceeded to test and adjust recipes that were candidates for publication in the book. Needless to say, the Webers ate a lot of gumbo in that two-year period.

In selecting the recipes for *The Louisiana Gumbo Cookbook*, the Webers made an effort to choose the best-tasting, most popular Cajun and Creole gumbo recipes in existence—the ones for which south Louisiana food is world-famous. The number of recipes fitting this description was more than the book could accommodate, so they began reducing the number by the process of elimination. Some recipes were eliminated because certain ingredients would be difficult or impossible to find outside of Louisiana. Others were cut because of excessive duplication in their particular category.

The net result, we believe, is the most complete cookbook on authentic Louisiana gumboes in existence today.

—TRENT ANGERS
Editor & Publisher

About the Authors

Floyd and Bea Weber

Bea and Floyd Weber are natives of the Cajun country in south Louisiana, now residing in Abbeville. They grew up on south Louisiana food, and they both enjoy cooking as a hobby today.

Bea learned the techniques of Cajun cooking from her family, descendants of Alexandre and Joseph Broussard (dit Beausoleil) of Acadie (now Nova Scotia), the ancestral homeland of the French-Acadian, or Cajun, people.

Floyd is a retired U.S. Air Force Officer, having spent most of his career in the Air Force Intelligence Command. He graduated with honors from Arizona State University and received an MBA from the University of Texas Graduate School of Business.

The Webers have resided in Japan, Texas, Arizona, Alaska and Pennsylvania. Their travels have taken them to most of the states and to several countries worldwide. They have two children and five grandchildren.

Table of Contents

Acknowledgements

The authors express their appreciation to food editor Amanda Griffin, who provided technical oversight and editing of the recipes included in this book. In every case, her effort resulted in an improved recipe, which provided more clarity to the reader.

We are also grateful to the publisher and editor, Trent Angers, and his professional staff at Acadian House. The countless hours they poured into the project made this the first-class book that gumbo deserved.

Finally, we thank everyone who were so gracious as to permit us to use their material in this book. Included are some excellent recipes which have been developed by these terrific cooks and chefs.

—B. & F.W.

Dedication

This book is dedicated to the parents of the authors: Mr. and Mrs. Isaac Broussard, Bea's parents; and Oklan Weber and Marie Landry Broussard, Floyd's parents.

The *Louisiana* GUMBO COOKBOOK

GUMBO: The Cajun and Creole Delicacy

Gumbo is the most famous of all south Louisiana foods. It is the best-known Cajun and Creole dish, and certainly one of the tastiest.

Gumbo is the one word that people around the world associate most with exquisite Louisiana cooking.

A good gumbo begins with a good roux, continues with chopped and sautéed vegetables, is followed by liquids as simple as water or as complex as seafood stock, and concludes with the addition of chicken, sausage, fish, shrimp, oysters, crabs, beef, turkey, duck or rabbit, or any combination of these.

It's versatile and flexible, it's delicious and nutritious, it can be eaten as a main course or served as an appetizer. And it can be frozen for later use.

Gumbo is not so hard to make. In fact, preparing gumbo is an easy and relaxing task, so long as you follow the instructions and allow enough time to do it right.

Louisiana gumbo is in no way a fast food item; it's a slow food. It requires tender loving care and an unhurried pace, enough time for the ingredients to blend one into the other to create that taste that is well worth waiting for. Rome wasn't built in a day, and a classic Louisiana gumbo cannot be whipped up in a hurry.

Why, even the creation of the first gumbo and its evolution into the dish we know today took a couple of centuries and maybe more. Nor was gumbo created by a single individual from a single country. Indeed, it took many people through many generations from several ethnic groups to create this masterpiece of international cuisine, namely, the Africans, the American Indians, the French, the French-Acadians and the Spaniards.

While there is an abundance of evidence pointing to the multi-ethnic character of gumbo, the body of written research on the origins and preparations of gumbo is quite limited. Presented here are some of those writings that are designed to define gumbo and illuminate its origins and its evolution into the popular meal that we know today.

Gumbo defined

For openers, Webster's Dictionary defines gumbo, or gombo, as "a soup thickened with okra pods and usually containing vegetables with meat or seafoods." It is also defined as "a mixture or melange." The word is of Bantu origin; it is "akin to Umbundu *ochinggombo* okra." The dictionary's first definition for gumbo is simply "okra."

The origins
of Louisiana Gumbo

In research conducted by home economist and author Louise Hanchey and reported in her work, *How We Cooked: Some Old Louisiana Recipes*, published in 1976, it is noted that the word "gumbo" stems from the African word for "okra" in any of several dialects. In the Belgian Congo the word for "okra" is " *tsingombo*;" in the Congo, " *qkuingombo*;" and in Angola "*otsingombo*" and "*kingombo*."

Hanchey reports that there is speculation that slaves brought the seeds of the okra plant with them in their hair. So okra, which was widely grown and used in Africa, was probably introduced to the New World by slaves. Okra is an ingredient which played a major part in the development of gumbo.

In Hanchey's research of the earliest literature on the subject, she finds that in Lafcadio Hearn's *La Cuisine Creole*, published in 1885, there is a recipe for Okra or Gombo, while in *The Creole Cookery Book*, published in the same year by the New Orleans Christian Women's Exchange, there are two recipes for Okra Soup which use the same ingredients mentioned by Hearn. Hanchey speculates that perhaps this is how gumbo became a soup.

"If anyone asked the African cooks what they were preparing, they probably answered with the word for okra," she writes.

There is also written evidence of gumbo being served in Louisiana as early as 1803. In his book, titled *Voyage to Louisiana, 1803-1805*, C.C. Robin mentions a type of soup called gumbo, and he points out that a cornmeal mush was served with the dish.

The epitome of Cajun
or Creole foods

In her book titled *Cajun-Creole Cooking*, Terry Thompson portrays gumbo as the most famous of all Louisiana foods. She writes:

> If I were asked to name one dish that epitomized Cajun or Creole food—worldwide—it would have to be gumbo. A simmering pot of gumbo embodies all of the rich and mysterious,

complex and spicy tastes of the cuisine.

Gumbo, like so many of our wonderful dishes, can be created from whatever is available. This can vary from the most meager combination of greens, possibly with a tiny piece of pork; to tough and otherwise unusable cuts of beef; to the richest sea-food-laden concoction affordable.

Gumbo is sublime. Indeed, one of my favorite meals is a spinach salad, a steaming bowl of gumbo, french bread and a glass of red wine. . . .

A few words of advice before you tackle the recipes. Good stocks are the basis for soups. If you start with a weak stock, you will have a weak soup. Of course, a bad stock will produce nothing good. Master the three stocks. . . and your soups, gumboes and bisques will have great foundations. Use canned stocks only if you must. Taste your soups carefully before salt-ing, especially those made from canned stocks. Remember that the only way to duplicate the complex depth of taste so charac-teristic of Cajun-Creole soups, gumboes and bisques is to use good homemade stocks.

Okra and filé powder are added to gumbo both for their taste and for their inherent thickening qualities. Both, however, break down with excessive cooking, resulting in a pot of stringy, vis-cous gumbo. Add sliced okra to the gumbo about 20 minutes before serving; cook just until tender. When reheating an okra gumbo, cook just to heat all of the ingredients thoroughly.

Filé powder should be added to the individual serving bowl, one-quarter to one-half teaspoon each, depending on personal preference and bowl size. If you add it to the whole pot of gumbo, do not reboil.

So now you're ready to haul out the big pots and simmer away. But don't be surprised if the neighbors show up for sup-per, having been lured by the aromas wafting from your kitchen.

Spanish, French and African all contributed to gumbo

An historical perspective on gumbo is provided in the writings of Morton G. Clark. In his book titled *French-American Cooking From New Orleans to Quebec*, he offers these insights:

Of all the marvelous Creole dishes created in the early days of Louisiana, none even closely approached the gumbo for fare. As made in its native habitat, gumbo stood about midway be-tween soup and stew (though it was always served as a soup).

And its proper consistency was indicated by its name, which came from the Bantu word *kingombo*, meaning okra. Okra in any dish gives it a special thickness, and okra in the early days was probably always an ingredient of the dish that took its name.

Later its place was often taken by a native powder, made from ground young sassafras leaves, called filé.

But there were times when neither okra nor filé was used, and the thick consistency was achieved instead by the use of pureed greens—beet tops, turnip tops, kale, cabbage, spinach, lettuce—as in the famous Gumbo Z'Herbes. Or both okra and filé might be used together.

A gumbo made with filé whether or not with okra, was almost always called a gumbo filé so there would be no mistake about the matter; gumbo made simply with okra was just a gumbo.

Where the idea for the dish came from is anybody's guess. The assortment of things that went into it in the way of meat and fowl and shellfish makes me feel that it was rather more of a Spanish idea than French; the somehow earthy blend of flavors I am sure was African. But the way of the dish, the method of its cookery was (and is) entirely French.

A good gumbo must proceed step by step. It starts with heated lard and then a brown roux; then the onions are browned with ham (if ham is used); then vegetables go into the dish and liquid is added and there follows the long, slow cooking to reduce the whole to the desired consistency. At last shellfish are added, unless filé is called for, in which case addition of the filé is the ultimate step. Filé should be added just at the moment the gumbo is taken from the fire. It should never be cooked. It is simply stirred into hot liquid, which it thickens immediately. If it is cooked, it will turn the soup or stew to stringy glue.

In some households in the old days the filé powder was actually added by each diner to his own plateful of gumbo at the table . . . . The gumbo, as one would expect (what with all the marvelous things that went into it) was often a dish of great elegance . . . . But it could be a dish of great thrift as well.

The development
of traditional Cajun cooking

In a report given to the 1992 assembly of the Attakapas Historical Association, Mathé Allain of the University of Southwestern Louisiana outlined the evolution of Louisiana Cajun and Creole cuisine. Ms. Allain reported that traditional Cajun cooking developed in the late eighteenth and early nineteenth centuries from a base provided by a French culinary tradition already modified by a hundred years of life in what is known today as Nova Scotia, the ancestral homeland of today's Cajuns. That base the Acadians transformed by borrowing from the ethnic groups they encountered in Louisiana—the Indians, the Spaniards, the Blacks and the French Creoles—and by adapting to the new game, new fish and new vegetables they found in south Louisiana. "Adaptability," which has always characterized Cajun cooks, had now blossomed into inventiveness and creativity, she pointed out.

She also had this to say on the subject:

> Okra Gumbo was prepared in the summer, filé gumbo the rest of the year. On Sundays, a chicken, probably in gumbo, was considered a special meal. The diet was based on availability: what could be grown, gathered, raised, fished or hunted. And the cooking was based on convenience: what could be set on the fire and left to simmer while the woman tended to her household chores and her field work.
>
> Seafood, so inextricably bound with Cajun tradition in the popular mind, historically was eaten only by those who lived close to the source. Thus, there are almost no oyster recipes in the traditional prairie and bayou Cajun cuisine. Oysters were New Orleans and coastal fare. Shrimp are seldom mentioned until the late nineteenth century, and then almost only in gumbo.
>
> The dependence on locally available ingredients produced regional differences. Interesting geographic variations appear in something as standard as chicken gumbo. The bayou Cajuns make it with chicken and andouille; in land-locked Evangeline Parish, it is made with chicken and sausage. Closer to the coast and its cornucopia of seafood, it becomes chicken and oysters.

Creole Gumbo,
"La Soupe Divine"

The colorful story behind the Creole Gumbo served in New Orleans is discussed by Howard Mitcham in his book, *Creole Gumbo And All That Jazz*. He writes:

> Creole Gumbo has deep and diverse roots and many ancestors. It's descended from the French peasant's *pot-au-feu* and the fisherman's *bouillabaisse*, from the communal pot of okra stew simmering on the tribal fire in an African village, and from the boiling pot of crabs and shrimp tended by Choctaw Indians on the north shore of Lake Pontchartrain (northeast of New Orleans).
>
> Gumbo is a mystique. Like jazz and the blues, it has overtones of voodoo, mumbo-jumbo, and the shaman's secret ritual. But best of all, it just tastes good. It's a one-dish meal, nourishing and filling, and it sticks to your ribs. Oh, it's just impossible to describe it. You'll have to come on down to New Orleans to try it.
>
> There are as many ways to make gumbo as there are cooks. No two cooks make it just alike, and for that matter, no cook makes it exactly the same way twice. It's an improvisational

thing, like early jazz. You just take off with whatever tune is handy, and then you travel . . . .

A Creole cook can take a handful of chicken wings or a turkey carcass or a piece of sausage or a few shrimp and crabs and whip up a gumbo. There are seafood gumbos, chicken gumbos, wild duck and squirrel gumbos, meat and sausage gumbos, okra and filé gumbos, and even a Lenten gumbo called Gumbo Z'Herbes, in which seven different types of greens are used.

All gumbos have two things in common: They all start off with a roux, and they all use either okra or filé as a thickening and flavoring agent. Bloody arguments and duels have been fought over whether okra or filé makes the best gumbo. The adherents of each school simply refuse to listen to those of the other . . . .

An Economical Meal

Aside from its preeminent position as a culinary success, the gumbo dish offers today's homemaker, as it did in the past, the added advantage of being a flexible dollar-stretcher.

How does this soup-stew concoction achieve flexibility and economic savings simultaneously? The wide diversity of recipes which exist and the plethora of variations which have been documented—virtually one per every cook—is indicative that cooks, in the city, country and home, have adapted the cookery to what was available in their area of domicile, what was available at the time, what was in season, or what the budget could handle on that day.

The meal is also flexible in terms of combinations of things. Gumbo is also versatile when you consider that it can be served as an appetizer but has enough character to be served as a main course.

The quick pace of today's society has generated an appetite for fast foods. Gumbo, which generally takes several hours to prepare, is not traditionally catalogued as a fast food item. But, possibly it should be. The busy housewife who has a job away from the home should make the mental note that gumbo improves with age and preserves well as a frozen food which can be quickly defrosted and heated to be served as a magnificent and tasty dish . . . .

Gumbo can become your "gourmet dinner in reserve" for that unscheduled crisis when the time schedule falls apart and there's no time left to prepare dinner. Prepare gumbo on a slow weekend on a planned basis when you determine that you have plenty of time. Freeze the gumbo in portions to be served, then relax, with the comfortable thought that you are a short moment away from a grand dinner even if you get in a time squeeze or if that unexpected company drops in on you close to meal time.

Gumbo is an excellent menu choice for serving a large crowd. Because it can be prepared in advance, it frees the host to mingle with the guests. Frequently, in casual settings, the large gumbo pot sits on the stove, and the guests serve themselves at their convenience. It's an excellent choice for the after-the-game get-together, the club gathering or the church social.

Gumbo is also economical in the sense that one can serve a large group without having to spend a substantial amount of money. An old Cajun expression hints at adding more stock to the gumbo when the unexpected visitor drops in without notice. One writer estimates the cost of a serving at only 90 cents per serving for the lessor complicated chicken gumboes.

A good gumbo appetizer can also support a less costly meal, and the guests will appreciate both. Served in this manner, the gumbo adds dimension as a course to a meal which might otherwise be on the plain side.

"Gumbo Weather"

A common saying heard in south Louisiana is the expression, "It's gumbo weather." Translated, this remark indicates that the temperature is cool. It is usually said on a cold, rainy day with grey clouds overhead. It's a day when you want to stay in and be cozy; and, you want to have a good time fellowshipping with friends. The expression is used most frequently in the wintertime but is also used on occasions in the summer . . . .

The foregoing represents a substantial part of the limited body of research on the dish called gumbo. Its origins are sketchy; its development is vague. Unlike the case where Chef Paul Prudhomme's blackened red fish became a classic with a known creator at a set point in time, gumbo remains a haunting melody with an uncertain beginning, an unknown author, but certainly one which has been enriched by time.

—Researched and compiled by Floyd Weber

Filé ... to spice up
your gumbo

Filé, the well-known herb traditionally used by the Cajuns and Creoles to spice up their gumboes, was originated by the Choctaw Indians of Louisiana.

Pronounced "fee-lay," the herb is made from dried sassafras leaves that have been pounded into a powder.

The history and usage of filé are discussed in a book by Howard Mitcham titled *Creole Gumbo And All That Jazz*. In the book, he describes filé as "the herb of all herbs among both Creoles and Cajuns." He also has this to say on the subject:

> For hundreds of years the Choctaw Indians have had a settlement at Bayou Lacombe on the north shore of Lake Pontchartrain (northeast of New Orleans). And they had a way of making gumbo long before the white man and the black man arrived. They invented filé, which is the product produced from the tender green leaves of the sassafras tree being gathered, dried and ground to a powder.
>
> A few tablespoons of the powder will thicken a whole pot of gumbo and give it a flavor that's spicy and pleasant. The filé should be added only after the pot is removed from the fire. Otherwise, if allowed to boil with the filé in it, the gumbo becomes stringy and unpalatable. Okra and filé should never be used together in a gumbo or it will be as thick as mud.
>
> The early Creoles in New Orleans used filé only in the wintertime, when fresh okra was not available, but many Cajuns of that era preferred filé gumbo year-round. They passed a bowl of filé around at the table, so that all the guests could take as much as they wanted.
>
> The Indians also supplied dried bay leaves (laurel), an essential flavoring element in most Creole soups and stews. At the old French Market near the river in New Orleans there were always several Choctaws sitting in the shade of the arcade, peddling their small caches of filé and dried bundles of bay leaves ....
>
> Today, filé of commercial grade can be purchased at most any grocery store in south Louisiana and at many other stores throughout the country. But the homemade kind is stronger and tastier .... You can make it yourself by pounding dried sassafras leaves with pestle and mortar. And while you're at it, pound up a few bay leaves for a terrific flavoring element.

The art of making a good roux

To an experienced Cajun or Creole cook, making a roux for a gumbo is a simple process that becomes second nature after a-while. But, to one who is not versed in the art of preparing a good roux, it can be a real mystery.

But, take heart! It's a simple mystery, a procedure that can be learned and that will work nearly every time if you are patient, if you follow the rules, and if you watch carefully what you're doing.

A roux is simply a mixture of fat and flour, cooked slowly and stirred continuously until it reaches the color desired for the dish you are preparing. Making a roux usually takes from 10 to 30 minutes, though some French chefs insist that a properly prepared roux takes an hour or more. Roux is also the most common and most critical ingredient that goes into a good Cajun or Creole gumbo. Virtually all Louisiana gumboes begin with a roux. So, needless to say, it is important to learn how to make one well if you are planning to prepare a gumbo.

Because of its importance in Cajun and Creole cooking, reams of copy on the preparation of the roux have been written by chefs and authors of cookbooks down through the years. Assembled here are the thoughts of three authors: Chef Earl Peyroux, writer of *Gourmet Cooking By Earl Peyroux*; Howard Mitcham, author of *Creole Gumbo And All That Jazz*; and Terry Thompson, writer of *Cajun-Creole Cooking*.

First, you make a roux

Earl Peyroux, in his book titled *Gourmet Cooking By Earl Peyroux*, discusses the preparation of basic roux and touches on some alternative means of achieving the same or similar results. His thoughts:

> Most French and Creole cooking either begins or ends with a sauce, and most good sauces begin with a roux. Ask most old-time cooks in New Orleans how to prepare a particular dish and you will most likely hear, "First, you make a roux . . . ."
>
> But if you are not an old-time New Orleans cook you may not know how to make a roux or . . . you may not even know what a roux is. A roux is the cooking of a quantity of flour in a fat over low heat, which prepares the particles of flour to absorb the

liquid used in the recipe, eliminates the raw pasty taste uncooked flour gives to a sauce, imparts a unique flavor to the dish . . . and acts as a thickening agent.

That's a lot for a little flour and butter.

A "light" roux is the basis of the classic cream sauces so common in French cooking, while a "dark" roux imparts a dark brown color and roasted nut-like flavor to gumbos, bisques, stews and dishes *"a la Creole . . . ."*

A dark roux is made several different ways. The fat is melted in a heavy skillet or sauce pan, which distributes the heat evenly, on a low to medium heat. The flour is then added and the stirring begins. A large kitchen spoon is best for this chore. Stirring constantly, cook the flour in the fat slowly. This will take from five to fifteen minutes until the desired color is achieved. Don't be timid. Let the roux cook until the color is a dark brown. By using a low or medium heat and stirring constantly you will avoid burning the flour. When the roux is done it can be used immediately . . . or it can be . . . stored in the refrigerator for several weeks.

Some cooks prepare a "dry" roux for later use. Flour is placed in a dry skillet or sauce pan and cooked over low heat, stirring constantly until the flour is a dark brown color. No fat is used at this time. The roux is then stored in a container until needed. When the "dry" roux is used, it is added to an equal part of melted fat and the recipe is continued from that point.

Making a roux is a simple but important technique in the preparation of French and Creole cooking. A little experience will make it "second nature," and before long you will be telling others, "First, you make a roux."

At one time the only accepted method for making a roux was to prepare it when ready to make that special dish. But now, the "dry roux" is growing in popularity, especially with the working wife who rushes in after a day at the office to prepare a meal for her family. The dry roux can be fixed well in advance of meal preparation, so the working person is able to save time by having the roux prepared beforehand. The microwave method of preparing roux is also gaining acceptance with many busy housewives. And in the South, commercially prepared roux is readily available in many supermarkets.

The key ingredient
of a good gumbo

Writing in his book, *Creole Gumbo And All That Jazz*, Howard Mitcham states flatly that the single most important flavoring element in both Creole and Cajun cooking is neither a spice nor an herb, but the roux. He explains:

The roux is the soul essence of most Creole-Cajun cooking. It's a subject that mystifies the uninitiated, but it's really very simple. To a Louisiana cook, making a roux comes as natural as breathing. "Roux" comes from the French term *"roux beurre,"* which means reddish-brown butter, and that's exactly what it is—flour or cornstarch browned with butter or other fat, shortening, or vegetable oil. The roux was used for centuries in French cookery for thickening sauces, soups and gravies, but it was regarded as peasant stuff by the masters of haute cuisine, who preferred the classic brown sauce.

It wasn't until the roux reached the New World that it became the backbone of a whole new cuisine. When the Creole, Cajun and Black cooks of New Orleans took hold of the delicate French roux, they whammed it and whacked it until it became something alive, strong and vibrant—a perfect backdrop for cooking the seafood, game and vegetables that were available in their region.

The chief function of a roux is to contribute a deep, resonant, browned flavor to any dish it's used in, and it thickens the dish and gives it body. Some of the things it does are almost metaphysical. It makes food slide gently down the tongue, and it tickles the taste buds as it passes by. For some mysterious reason, a good roux inhibits spoiling or souring of a soup or stew.

There are still two schools of thought on roux-making. Many aristocratic Creoles think a light golden-colored roux is best. But most Cajun and Black cooks prefer a roux that's dark brown, as rich a hue as you can get it without scorching or burning it. The latter type has a very pronounced and recognizable flavor.

The great Escoffier thought the dark brown peasant style of roux, made with flour, was indigestible, and he went to great lengths to explain why a cook should use cornstarch instead of flour. If he had come down to Thibodaux, La., talking like that, they would have ridden him out of town on a rail! When a good cook uses them, either method is satisfactory.

Only a serenely patient cook should try to make a roux. A jumpy, nervous person will scorch or burn it every time. Our instructions here call for butter, but you can use clarified bacon drippings, lard, shortening, vegetable oil, or even olive oil.

To make an average-size roux, melt a half stick (four tablespoons) of butter in a heavy skillet over low heat, add four tablespoons of flour, and stir it in until the mixture is creamy and free of lumps. Turn the heat very low and continue to stir, scraping the bottom of the skillet, for at least 25 minutes.

When a roux reaches its climax and is done, it begins to brown very rapidly and you must be on your toes to keep it under control and not let it scorch or burn. If it does, you must throw it out, clean the skillet perfectly, and start all over again—a very tedious business. Some perfectionist aficionados of the art, using very, very low heat and lots of patience, can carry a roux for an hour or more before it reaches maturity, and they swear that this is the best roux of all.

When you've brought your roux to the shade of brown you want, you can set it aside until you're ready to use it, or you can add onions, green onions, bellpeppers—whatever vegetables and seasonings the particular recipe calls for—to the roux in the skillet and keep on cooking until the vegetables are soft and transparent, but not browned.

Many cooks make roux in large amounts and freeze it in small individual packets, so that they won't have to go through this complex rigamarole every time they cook.

Roux is hot,
so be careful!

In her book, *Cajun-Creole Cooking*, Terry Thompson reminds the cook to be careful not to spill or splash roux on the skin, as it is hot, hot, hot! She offers these words to the wise:

When stirring and handling the roux, be extremely careful not to splash any of it on your skin. Roux sticks to the skin and can cause a very serious burn.

If you are preparing a larger quantity of roux, use a pan large enough to hold all of the fat and flour and allow enough room for stirring or whisking without splash-overs.

The choice of a stirring implement is a personal one. I find that a long-handled metal whisk covers more of the pan surface. If you are more comfortable with spoons, then use a wooden spoon. Metal spoons become extremely hot during the long cooking process.

Even after the roux has been removed from the pan to a metal bowl, you must still be very careful with it. Do not set the bowl on a polyethylene or plastic cutting board or on your plastic laminate counter top. These materials will melt and burn. Remember that you are dealing with a substance that is in excess of 500 degrees fahrenheit!

The preparation of a roux has developed into something of an art form down through the years. Happily, though, it is an art that one can learn with relative ease. Toward that end, a number of recipes for making roux are presented on the following pages.

ROUX

Roux

1 1/2 cups of cooking oil

1 1/2 cups of flour

1. Heat oil in a heavy skillet over medium heat. (A black cast-iron skillet is frequently used.)

2. Add the flour in small amounts while stirring continuously. When the roux reaches a light brown color, lower the heat.

3. Continue to cook until the roux is the color of dark chocolate. (This process will take about 30 minutes, but old-timers insist that "a real roux" takes a minimum of one hour to prepare.)

Note: The roux plays a most important part in the success of the gumbo, and is the basis of the dish. Don't commit good gumbo ingredients to a roux that is poorly made or one that is burned. Instead, throw the roux away, clean the skillet thoroughly, then start over, because a burnt roux will give gumbo a bitter taste.

If you haven't mastered the making of a roux on the stove top, you might try the easier alternatives of a store-bought (commercially prepared) roux, microwave roux, or oven-baked roux.

If you are in a time bind, prepare your roux in advance and store it in the refrigerator. This will save you considerable time on the day you begin to prepare the gumbo. If you can master this part of the preparation, making gumbo will fall in place for you.

Bea Weber
Abbeville, La.

22

Basic Roux
(To Be Prepared In Advance)

1. Combine oil and flour in a large, heavy skillet; stir until smooth and blended.

2. Cook over low heat, stirring frequently, until roux is the dark brown color of pecan shells, about an hour.

3. Remove from heat and cool completely. Pour into air-tight containers and refrigerate or freeze until ready to use.

4. Thaw roux at room temperature; stir well before using.

Makes about three cups.

Debbie Maugans Barton
"Make-Ahead Roux
    For Quick Cajun Cooking"
Creative Ideas For Living

---

3 cups of vegetable oil

---

3 cups of all-purpose flour

Cajun Roux

1 cup of lard

1 cup of all-purpose flour

No respectable Cajun household would be without a good supply of roux. When you prepare roux, make a little extra; it freezes well in one-cup containers.

1. Melt lard in a heavy Dutch oven or a 12-inch skillet over medium heat. When lard is hot, add flour all at once; stir or whisk quickly to combine flour and lard. If necessary, use the back of a wooden spoon to smooth out any lumps of flour.

2. Reduce heat to low. Cook, stirring or whisking constantly, until roux is desired color and has a nut-like smell.

3. Cook about 45 minutes for peanut butter-colored roux or 55 minutes for the dark mahogany-colored roux.

Makes one cup.

VARIATIONS:

Vegetable oil may be substituted but the taste of the finished dish will not be as rich as one pre-pared with a roux made with lard. Another fat, such as ren-dered duck fat, or a combination of duck fat and lard may be used.

Note: The roux process should not be rushed. If small black or dark-brown flecks appear in roux, it has been burned and must be discarded. A burned roux will impart a bitter and scorched taste to any dish in which it is used. To stop the cooking process, either add the vegetables called for in the recipe or immediately pour finished roux into a metal bowl. Stir or whisk 10 minutes in bowl. To make roux ahead of time, cover and refrigerate for two days or freeze up to six months.

Terry Thompson
Cajun-Creole Cooking

Smooth Roux

1 1/4 cups of safflower oil

2 1/4 cups of unbleached flour

1. In a large, heavy skillet, heat oil very hot.

2. Add one cup of flour; stir well until dissolved.

3. Add remaining flour; cook over medium heat, stirring constantly until reddish-brown in color.

4. Remove from heat; set skillet in cold water, stirring as roux cools.

Makes one and a half cups.

Note: This recipe is exceptionally good, as the safflower oil is so easily digested. This roux may be stored in the freezer in a closed container an indefinite length of time.

Teresa Hicks Bunetta
*Acadiana French and American
Cuisine Seasoned With His Love*

Bake-A-Roux

1. Mix flour and oil together in a thick pot or pan with no-burn handle.

2. Put into oven on center shelf.

3. Bake at 400 degrees for one and a half to two hours, or more if you like it real brown.

4. Stir the mixture every 15 minutes or so.

5. When cool, store in jars in refrigerator for future use.

Mrs. Ira Miller
Quelque Chose Piquant

2 quarts of flour

1 quart of cooking oil

Fat-Free Roux

1 cup of all-purpose flour

Method 1:

Place flour in a cast iron skillet. Bake at 400 degrees, stirring occasionally, until dark brown, about 30 to 40 minutes.

Method 2:

Place flour in a cast iron skillet; cook over medium heat, stirring constantly, until flour is dark brown, for 25 to 30 minutes.

Method 3:

1. Place flour in a glass casserole.

2. Microwave on high for two minutes; stir well.

3. Repeat microwaving flour in one-minute increments, stirring well, until flour is dark brown. (Repeat two to four times, as needed.)

Yield: one cup.

Louisiana Farm Bureau Women
Foods a la Louisiana

Microwave Roux

The greatest thing about making a roux in the microwave oven is that stirring is practically eliminated. You can use the extra time to chop seasonings.

1. Use an uncovered two-quart glass dish (oven-proof). Blend together flour and oil.

2. Cook in microwave oven on high for 10 minutes. The color of the roux should be a deep caramel.

3. Roux does not look good at this point; the flour is still gritty and the fat is still a little separated. But don't worry! Stir-in seasonings such as onion, celery and bellpepper. Sauté for three minutes on high. Note that the color has deepened and the roux is shiny.

4. Stir-in green onions, parsley and garlic and sauté on high for two additional minutes. This is the basis for many brown gravies and most Creole gravies.

Note: Using a larger quantity or larger utensil will affect cooking time, as will a smaller utensil or quantity. I judge by color, along with time.

Jeanne H. Landry
Sauté. A Collection Of Creole Recipes For The Microwave Oven

1/2 cup of oil

1/2 cup of flour

RICE

Rice I

Rice has been part of the tradi-tional American meal since it was first grown in the U.S. more than 300 years ago. And during this time, some masterful recipes have turned up in our country's differ-ent regional and cultural pockets.

For best results, always follow package directions. When direc-tions are not available, use this easy method:

1. Combine one cup of rice, liquid (see chart, below), one teaspoon of salt (optional), and one table-spoon of butter or margarine (optional) in a two- to three-quart saucepan.

2. Heat to boiling; stir once or twice.

3. Lower heat to simmer; cover with tight-fitting lid. Cook according to time specified on chart. If rice is not quite tender or liquid is not absorbed, replace lid and cook for two to four min-utes longer.

4. Fluff with fork.

USA Rice Council

1 cup of uncooked rice	Liquid	Cooking time
Regular-milled long grain	1 3/4 to 2 cups	15 minutes
Regular-milled medium or short grain	1 1/2 cups	15 minutes
Brown	2 to 2 1/2 cups	45 to 50 minutes
Parboiled	2 to 2 1/2 cups	20 to 25 minutes
Precooked	Follow package directions	
Flavored or seasoned mixes	Follow package directions	

Rice II

1. Put all ingredients in a two-quart saucepan and bring to a boil.

2. Lower heat to medium and cook until water and rice are at the same level.

3. Cover, lower heat to low, and cook about 20 minutes. Taste to determine that rice is sufficiently cooked.

Bea Weber
Abbeville, La.

1 cup of white rice

2 cups of water

1 teaspoon of salt

1 teaspoon of vinegar or lemon juice (to whiten the rice)

STOCK

Brown Veal & Pork Stock

8 pounds of veal bones
and knuckles, cut in half

4 pounds of veal shoulder and
shanks

5 pigs' feet, cut in half

6 onions, coarsely chopped

3 carrots, coarsely chopped

3 celery stalks, coarsely chopped

1 6-ounce can of tomato paste

6 thyme sprigs or 2 teaspoons of
dried thyme

2 bay leaves

Parsley stems

1 tablespoon of peppercorns

The use of pork bones in a veal stock may seem a very radical thing to non-Southerners, but the flavor derived from this is marvelous and is right at home in the hearty dishes of south Louisiana. If you cannot find pigs' feet, substitute four pounds of pork neck bones.

1. Preheat oven to 425.

2. Place all bones, meat and pigs' feet in large roasting pans. Brown in preheated oven until very dark, but not burned, turning often. This takes about two hours. (Melting fat will create a lot of smoke in the oven. If too much melted fat collects in the pan during cooking, skim it off, using a non-plastic bulb baster. Do not let it overflow into the oven.)

3. Place browned bones in a 15- to 20-quart stockpot.

4. Leave a thin film of fat in one pan; pour off and discard fat from pans. Place onions, carrots and celery in pan with thin film of fat; spread evenly. Cook in preheated oven, stirring frequently, until well-browned.

5. Add browned vegetables and tomato paste to stockpot.

6. Pour off all remaining fat from pan; place pan over high heat.

Add one cup of water to pan to deglaze, scraping up all browned bits from pan bottom. Repeat with remaining pans.

7. Add browned mixture to stockpot. Add enough water to stockpot to completely cover bones and vegetables by about two inches.

8. Bring to a full boil, skimming grey foam from surface often. Continue boiling until no more foam forms. Reduce heat.

9. Add remaining seasonings; simmer 10 hours.

10. Cool slightly. Strain three times through a fine strainer or cheesecloth. Pour into shallow pans; cool to room temperature in sink of cold water. Refrigerate until chilled. Remove all fat from surface.

11. Pour into quart containers; seal. Refrigerate up to two days or freeze up to six months.

Makes 8 to 10 quarts.

Terry Thompson
Cajun-Creole Cooking

Louisiana Brown Poultry Stock

10 to 12 pounds of uncooked mixed poultry bones and carcasses, such as chicken, duck, game hen, quail, dove and turkey

2 carrots, coarsely chopped

2 large onions, unpeeled, coarsely chopped

1 large leek, coarsely chopped

1 celery stalk with leafy top, coarsely chopped

6 parsley sprigs

6 thyme sprigs or 2 teaspoons of dried leaf thyme

1 bay leaf

The secret to the greatness of this stock is the use of as many types of poultry bones as possible. And be sure that you have duck bones in there, as they add a wonderful flavor.

1. Preheat oven to 425. Place all bones and carcasses in large roasting pans. Brown bones and carcasses in oven until very dark, but not burned, turning often. This takes about two hours. (Do not burn the bones, or the stock will have a very bitter taste.)

2. Place browned bones in a 20-quart stockpot.

3. Leaving a thin film of fat in one pan, pour off and discard fat from pans. Place carrots, onions, leek and celery in pan with thin film of fat, spreading evenly. Cook in preheated oven, stirring frequently, until well-browned.

4. Add browned vegetables to stockpot.

5. Pour off all remaining fat from pan; place pan over high heat. Add one cup of water to pan to deglaze, scraping up all browned bits from pan bottom. Repeat with remaining pan. Add browned mixture to stockpot.

6. Add enough water to stockpot to completely cover bones and vegetables by about two inches.

7. Bring to a boil; skim grey foam from the surface often. Boil until no more foam forms.

8. Reduce heat; add seasonings. Simmer eight hours. Skim fat from surface occasionally.

9. Cool slightly. Strain stock three times through a fine strainer or cheesecloth; discard bones and vegetables.

10. Pour into shallow pans; cool in sink of cold water to room temperature. Refrigerate until chilled. Remove all fat from surface.

11. Pour into quart containers; seal tightly. Refrigerate up to two days or freeze up to six months.

Makes 8 to 10 quarts.

Terry Thompson
Cajun-Creole Cooking

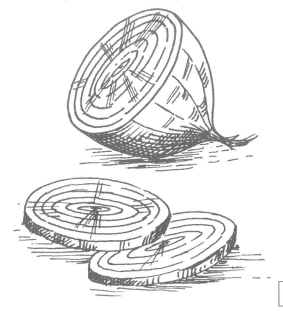

Seafood Stock

10 pounds of mixed shellfish shells or fish carcasses and bones

5 onions, unpeeled, quartered

1 tablespoon of whole cloves

2 celery stalks, coarsely chopped

5 garlic cloves, unpeeled, smashed

1 large lemon, sliced

1 3-ounce box of shrimp and crab boil

1 tablespoon of peppercorns

There is no truly acceptable substitute for real seafood stock, but if you simply must use an alternative, bottled clam juice is your best bet. Any type of non-oily, white-fleshed fish bones may be used, but avoid deep-sea fish or any fish with dark meat. Whenever possible, include whole crab carcassses and shrimp heads and shells. If you have crawfish shells and heads, they are an extra treat. The more varieties you use, the more complex the taste will be. A couple of big lobster carcasses would be sublime!

1. Place all ingredients in a 15- to 20-quart stockpot. Add enough water to cover by four inches. Bring to full boil over high heat.

2. Skim grey foam from surface; reduce heat. Simmer three hours.

3. Cool slightly. Strain three times through a fine strainer or cheesecloth; discard bones and vegetables.

4. Pour into shallow pans; cool in sink of cold water to room temperature. Refrigerate until chilled.

5. Remove all fat from surface.

6. Pour into quart containers; seal. Refrigerate up to two days or freeze up to six months.

Makes 8 to 10 quarts.

Terry Thompson
Cajun-Creole Cooking

BEEF & PORK

Seven Steak & Okra Gumbo

2 1/2 pounds of "Seven Steak" or "Seven Bone Steak" or beef neck chops

4 tablespoons of Chef Paul Prudhomme's Meat Magic ®

1/2 cup of pork lard, bacon fat, shortening or vegetable oil

1/2 cup of all-purpose flour

2 pounds of okra, sliced into 1/4-inch pieces (8 cups, sliced)

3 cups of chopped onion

2 tablespoons of unsalted butter

4 bay leaves

7 1/2 cups of beef stock

2 cups of chopped celery

2 cups of chopped bellpepper

2 cups of peeled and chopped tomatoes

2 tablespoons of chopped jalapeno peppers* (optional)

1 tablespoon of minced garlic

3/4 pound of peeled medium shrimp (optional)

3 cups of hot cooked rice

1. Cut meat into eight equal size pieces. Sprinkle meat with some of the Meat Magic mix, rubbing it into both sides of the meat by hand. Reserve leftover seasoning.

2. In a large, heavy skillet heat the pork lard. Meanwhile, combine 1 1/2 teaspoons of the Meat Magic with the flour in a pan; dredge meat in the seasoned flour. Brown meat on both sides in the hot lard. Remove from skillet and set aside.

3. Add four cups of the okra to the skillet. Fry over high heat until many okra slices are dark brown, about eight minutes, stirring occasionally.

4. Add one cup of the onion, the butter and two teaspoons of the Meat Magic. Cook over high heat four minutes, stirring frequently.

5. Add the bay leaves and half a cup of the stock; continue cooking for four minutes, stirring often. Add half a cup more stock (Along with frying, repeated additions of stock help break down the okra); cook five minutes, stirring occasionally and scraping pan bottom well if mixture starts to stick.

6. Add half a cup more stock and continue cooking for three minutes, stirring occasionally. Add the remaining two cups of onion, the celery, bellpepper and the remaining Meat Magic; stir well.

7. Cook for five minutes, stirring occasionally. Stir-in the tomatoes, jalapeno peppers (if desired) and garlic. Cook for five minutes, stirring occasionally.

8. Transfer mixture to a gumbo pot or large soup pot. Add the remaining six cups of stock and the meat. Cook uncovered over high heat for 10 minutes.

9. Add the remaining four cups of okra and lower heat to a simmer. Cook covered until meat is tender, about 20 minutes, being careful not to let the gumbo scorch.

10. Add shrimp (if desired), cover and remove from heat; let sit 10 minutes.

11. Serve immediately in bowls, allowing for each person about a third cup of rice, a portion of meat and one and a half cups of gumbo poured on top.

* Fresh jalapenos are preferred; if you have to use pickled ones, rinse as much vinegar from them as possible.

Makes eight main-course servings.

Paul Prudhomme
*Chef Paul Prudhomme's
Louisiana Kitchen*

Burgundy Beef Gumbo

1/2 cup of oil

1/4 cup of bacon drippings

1 cup of flour

2 pounds of lean beef

1 cup of onion

3 or 4 quarts of water

3 beef bouillon cubes

Salt, to taste

Pepper and Tabasco sauce, to taste

1/4 teaspoon of thyme

1/4 teaspoon of marjoram

2 cups of dry red wine

1. Heat oil and bacon drippings in a heavy pot; add flour and brown until flour is dark brown in color. Stir constantly.

2. Add beef and continue stirring until beef is well-coated with roux.

3. Add onion. Cook until onion is wilted.

4. Add water and bouillon cubes.

5. Simmer for 20 minutes.

6. Add salt, pepper, thyme, marjoram, wine and Tabasco.

7. Simmer 10 minutes.

8. Serve over hot cooked rice.

Bea Weber
Abbeville, La.

Beef Creole Gumbo

1. In heavy cast iron or cast aluminum pot, stir-fry onion, garlic, okra, oil and salt pork until well-mixed, about 10 to 15 minutes. Mixture will be slimy. Remove from pot.

2. Cook ground beef in pot, cooking slowly and breaking meat apart. Do not overcook.

3. Add tomatoes and press large chunks against sides of pot.

4. Add okra mixture and cans of water for thickness desired.

5. Add Worcestershire sauce, salt, black pepper and red pepper. Heat to high, reduce heat and simmer one hour.

6. Serve over hot rice.

Jeanette Pennell Doiron (Editor)
Food, Glorious Food

---

1 large onion, chopped

1 or 2 cloves of garlic, minced

1 pound of frozen chopped okra, thawed

1/4 cup of cooking oil

1/4 cup of minced salt pork

1 pound of ground beef (not hamburger)

1 1-pound can of tomatoes

1 to 3 cans of water

2 tablespoons of Worcestershire sauce

Salt, black pepper and cayenne (or red hot pepper sauce), to taste

Beef Brisket & Okra Gumbo

1-quart package of frozen okra, thawed

1 fresh tomato, cut up into small pieces

1/2 cup of oil

2 pounds of brisket or ribs, seasoned with salt and pepper and cut in 2-inch cubes

1 large onion, chopped

2 cloves of garlic, minced

3 quarts of water

1. Fry okra and tomato in oil until okra is not gummy; set aside.

2. Brown meat in gumbo pot until it is well-browned.

3. Add a little water; then add onion and garlic to meat.

4. Add three quarts of water and bring to a boil. Boil until meat is tender.

5. Add okra and tomato mixture to meat. Cook for 10 to 15 minutes.

6. Serve over hot cooked rice.

Mrs. Marie B. Broussard
Kaplan, La.

Beef Ribs & Okra Gumbo

1. In a large heavy pot, heat one-fourth cup of oil (Reserve remainder for later use in this recipe).

2. Brown ribs in oil.

3. Add water to the ribs; when water comes to a boil, lower heat and add bouillon; simmer.

4. Heat remaining oil in large pot; add okra, onions, garlic and tomatoes.

5. Cook vegetable mixture until okra has wilted and changed color slightly.

6. Add lemon juice. This will cut the gumminess.

7. Add okra mixture to beef and broth.

8. Add salt and pepper.

9. Turn heat up to medium and cook for 10 to 15 minutes.

10. Serve over hot cooked rice.

Bea Weber
Abbeville, La.

1/2 cup of vegetable oil

2 1/2 pounds of beef ribs

4 quarts of water (approximately)

4 beef bouillon cubes

2 1/2 pounds of fresh okra, washed, dried and sliced thin

1 large onion, chopped

4 cloves of garlic, minced

2 fresh tomatoes, peeled and quartered

1 tablespoon of lemon juice

Salt & pepper, to taste

Round Steak-Okra Gumbo

1/2 cup of vegetable oil, divided

3 pounds of lean round steak, cut into serving portions

2 cans of beef broth

4 quarts of water

3 pounds of okra, sliced into 1/2-inch pieces

1 1/2 cups of chopped onion

4 cloves of garlic, minced

2 fresh tomatoes, peeled and quartered

2 or 3 teaspoons of lemon juice

Salt and pepper, to taste

Tabasco sauce

1. In a large, heavy pot, heat one-fourth cup of oil.

2. Add round steak and brown.

3. Lower heat and add beef broth and water. Simmer.

4. In another heavy pot, heat remaining oil. Add okra, onion, garlic and tomatoes. Cook until okra has changed color and has wilted. Add lemon juice. (This will cut the gumminess of the okra).

5. Add vegetable mixture to beef and beef broth.

6. Add salt, pepper and Tabasco, to taste.

7. Serve over hot cooked rice.

Bea Weber
Abbeville, La.

Pork Roast Gumbo

Absolutely outstanding!

1. Boil pork roast in water seasoned with onion flakes and one teaspoon of the K's Cajun Seasoning until tender, about one and a half hours.

2. Remove meat to chopping board and when cool enough to handle cut meat from bone and then cut into very small pieces. Return the meat to the stock.

3. Make roux in iron pot with bacon drippings and flour, stirring over medium heat until cocoa brown. Stir-in onion; cook three minutes; add to stock pot.

4. In the same skillet, cook okra in melted butter about 10 minutes.

5. Add okra and all remaining ingredients (except filé) to stock and cook another hour.

6. Remove bay leaves. Serve over rice with filé.

Serves 12 to 15.

Note: Many Cajuns wouldn't dream of making a roux in anything but an iron skillet, which is ideal for evenly browning the flour.

Gwen McKee
The Little Gumbo Book

1 3-pound pork shoulder picnic roast or Boston butt roast

3 1/2 quarts of water

1 tablespoon of dried onion flakes

2 teaspoons of K's Cajun Seasoning (or salt and pepper), divided

3 tablespoons of bacon drippings

4 tablespoons of flour

1 1/2 cups of chopped onion

1/2 stick of butter or margarine

3 cups of cut okra

1 teaspoon of minced garlic

1 teaspoon of Tabasco sauce

1 teaspoon of brown sugar

2 bay leaves

1/2 pound of diced ham (optional)

Filé

Pork Tasso With Okra Gumbo

4 pounds of tasso, cut in small pieces

3 cups of okra (frozen)

2 quarts of water

1 cup of tomato sauce

1 cup of chopped onion

1 bellpepper, chopped

3 teaspoons of salt

1/4 teaspoon of pepper

A Grand Champion recipe

1. Smother tasso with the okra in a skillet for about 30 minutes.

2. Bring water to a boil in a large pot. Add the tasso and okra to the hot water along with the tomato sauce, onion, bellpepper, salt and pepper.

3. Simmer for two hours.

4. Serve with rice or crackers.

Note: This makes a large quantity of gumbo, and it is equally good reheated and served on another day.

Mrs. Oris Guidry
Quelque Chose Beaucoup Bon

SAUSAGE

Sausage-Okra Gumbo

1 1/2 pounds of smoked, country-style pork sausage

1 tablespoon of butter or margarine

3 tablespoons of flour

2 cups of chicken broth

1 18-ounce bag of frozen gumbo vegetables*

1 16-ounce can of tomatoes, chopped

1/4 teaspoon of garlic powder

1 1/2 teaspoons of salt

1/8 to 1/4 teaspoon of ground red pepper

2 teaspoons of filé

3 cups of hot cooked rice

1. Cover sausage with water and cook for 10 minutes in a covered Dutch oven. Drain; cut sausage into one-inch pieces and set aside.

2. Melt butter in Dutch oven. Add flour and cook, stirring, until mixture is deep brown.

3. Add broth, vegetables, tomatoes, garlic powder, salt, pepper and sausage. Bring to a boil; reduce heat, cover and simmer for 25 minutes.

4. Remove from heat; add filé. (Do not boil once filé has been added.)

5. Ladle gumbo into bowls and top with a scoop of rice.

Makes six entree servings or 10 appetizer servings.

USA Rice Council

* Or use a combination of okra, corn, onions, celery and sweet red pepper

Andouille, Sausage, Oyster & Smoked Turkey Gumbo

1. Heat oil in heavy pot. Add flour, stirring constantly over medium heat. Cook until flour is golden brown.

2. Add onion, celery, bellpepper and garlic. Sauté until onions are wilted.

3. Add water and liquid from oysters.

4. Add turkey, andouille, smoked sausage; stir to blend then simmer two hours.

5. Add oysters and water to retain volume.

6. Continue cooking until oysters curl.

7. Add parsley and green onion tops; cook five minutes longer.

8. Serve over hot cooked rice.

Bea Weber
Abbeville, La.

1 cup of oil

1 cup of flour

2 1/2 cups of chopped onion

1 cup of chopped celery

1 cup of chopped bellpepper

4 cloves of garlic, chopped fine

1 gallon of hot water

1 pint of oysters (reserve liquid)

Left over smoked turkey carcass and meat

1 pound of andouille

1/2 pound of smoked sausage

1/2 cup of chopped parsley

1/2 cup of chopped green onion tops

Andouille Gumbo

1 large hen, cut into serving pieces

1 cup of oil

1 cup of flour

2 large onions, chopped

2 cups of water

2 pounds of andouille, cut into 1-inch pieces

3 quarts of water

2 bottles of clam juice or chicken stock

2 1/2 teaspoons of Worcestershire sauce

3 tablespoons of Tabasco sauce

2 dozen oysters (optional)

Salt and cayenne pepper

1/2 cup of chopped onion tops

1/2 cup of chopped parsley

1 teaspoon of filé (optional)

1. Season hen with salt and cayenne; set aside.

2. In a large heavy pot make a roux by heating oil, then adding flour and stirring constantly until flour is dark brown in color.

3. Add onions to roux; stir until onions are wilted and are transparent.

4. Add hen to roux and onion mixture, stirring to coat meat with roux.

5. Add two cups of water to mixture.

6. Cook a few minutes, then add andouille.

7. Add three quarts of water and clam juice.

8. Bring to a boil, then lower heat; simmer for 1 1/2 hours.

9. Add Worcestershire sauce and Tabasco.

10. Add oysters.

11. Cook until oysters curl (about 15 minutes).

12. Taste for seasoning. Add salt and cayenne if needed.

13. Add onion tops and parsley.

14. Remove from heat and cover for five minutes.

15. Serve over hot cooked rice.

Andouille Filé Gumbo

1. Heat vegetable oil over medium heat; add flour, stirring constantly until flour is dark brown.

2. Add onion, bellpepper and celery, stirring constantly until onion is transparent.

3. Add andouille, Stock, gizzards, and three and a half quarts of water.

4. Bring to a boil on low to medium heat; cook for 60 minutes.

5. Taste for seasoning. Add salt and cayenne if desired.

6. Add chopped green onions and parsley. Cook three minutes.

7. In each serving bowl, add a fourth teaspoon of filé.

8. Add hot gumbo to the bowl and serve with hot cooked rice.

9. Add Tabasco.

1 cup of vegetable oil

1 cup of all-purpose flour

1 cup of chopped onions

1/4 cup of chopped bellpepper

1/4 cup of chopped celery

3 pounds of andouille sausage (cut in 1-inch pieces)

Stock (Recipe follows)

3 to 3 1/2 quarts of water

Salt and red cayenne pepper, to taste

1/2 cup of chopped green onions

1/2 cup of chopped parsley

Filé

Tabasco, to taste

STOCK

1. Rinse and season gizzards with salt and cayenne pepper.

2. Place in pan with one and a half quarts of water.

3. Boil gizzards until tender; set aside. Reserve the gizzards to place in the gumbo.

1 1/2 pounds of chicken gizzards

1 1/2 quarts of water

Salt & cayenne pepper

Bea Weber
Abbeville, La.

Gumbo Ya Ya

1/2 cup of oil

3 tablespoons of flour

1 pound of andouille sausage, cut into 1-inch pieces

1 medium onion, chopped

1 medium bellpepper, chopped

1 tablespoon of butter

2 cups of chicken stock

1 cup of diced chicken

Salt and pepper, to taste

2 teaspoons of filé

1/2 cup of water

1. Heat oil in a saucepan. Gradually add flour, stir continually and cook until flour turns a dark brown. Set aside.

2. In another saucepan, sauté andouille sausage, onion and bellpepper in butter for approximately 10 minutes.

3. Add chicken stock and simmer for 10 minutes. Let mixture come to a boil.

4. Add roux and let simmer for 20 minutes.

5. Add one cup of diced chicken.

6. Salt and pepper, to taste.

7. Dissolve filé in water. Add filé to gumbo at the last minute and simmer for 10 minutes.

8. Serve over hot rice.

Serves four.

Gerard Maras
Mr. B's Bistro
New Orleans, La.

CHICKEN

Chicken Gumbo

1 fryer, about 2 1/2 pounds,
cut into serving pieces

1/4 pound of smoked ham, diced

2 tablespoons of butter
or margarine

1 pound of sliced okra

1 14 1/2- to 16-ounce can of
whole peeled tomatoes, chopped

1 cup of sliced onion

3/4 cup of chopped bellpepper

1 tablespoon of snipped fresh
parsley

1 teaspoon of salt

1 small bay leaf

1/4 teaspoon of ground black
pepper

1 tablespoon of gumbo filé

4 cups of hot cooked rice

1. Cook chicken and ham in butter in large skillet until lightly browned.

2. Add okra, tomatoes, onion, bellpepper, parsley, salt, bay leaf, pepper, and six cups of water; heat to boiling.

3. Reduce heat, cover and simmer 30 to 40 minutes, or until chicken is tender.

4. Remove chicken from bones, but do not chop into small pieces.

5. Return chicken to gumbo. Discard bay leaf. Just before serving, sprinkle filé lightly over gumbo, stirring constantly.

6. Ladle gumbo into bowls and top with hot rice.

Makes eight servings (about three quarts).

USA Rice Council

Chicken or Shrimp Gumbo

1. Add flour to cooking oil in cold iron skillet on medium heat.

2. Stir constantly until flour is dark brown, being careful not to burn.

3. Add roux to boiling water.

4. Add chopped onion, celery, bellpepper and parsley.

5. Let boil 30 minutes before adding chicken.

6. About 10 minutes before chicken is done, add green onions.

7. When gumbo is done, season to taste and add filé.

8. Serve over hot rice with french bread.

9. Pepper sauce can be added to individual servings for extra taste.

Note: About four pounds of shrimp tails (weigh before peeling) may be substituted for chicken. Boil gumbo one hour before adding shrimp.

Mr. J.D. Morgan
Pots, Pans and Pioneers

3/4 cup of flour

1/2 cup of cooking oil

4 quarts of boiling water

1 large onion, chopped

2 stalks of celery, chopped

1/4 cup of chopped bellpepper

Few leaves of chopped parsley, or flakes

1 large hen, cut into serving pieces and seasoned

1 cup of green onions, chopped

Salt and pepper, to taste

1 tablespoon of filé

Chicken Filé Gumbo

1 hen, cut into serving pieces

Salt, black pepper and red pepper

1 cup of cooking oil

1/4 cup of flour

1 cup of chopped onion

1 cup of chopped celery

1/2 cup of chopped bellpepper

2 quarts of hot water

1 cup of chopped green onion tops

1/2 cup of chopped parsley

Filé

1. Season chicken with salt, black pepper and red pepper.

2. Heat oil in iron pot until hot. Add seasoned chicken and cook until golden brown.

3. Remove chicken, add flour to make a roux, add onion, celery, bellpepper and cook slowly until soft, about five minutes.

4. Add chicken and water. Simmer until tender.

5. Add green onion tops and parsley the last 15 or 20 minutes. When done, add filé, to taste. (Skim off surplus fat, if necessary).

6. Serve over rice.

Serves six.

Mrs. Nedia B. Hebert
Jeanerette, La.

Chicken & Okra Gumbo

1. Heat the lard in a soup kettle; when hot add the chicken and the ham.

2. Cover and let it simmer ten minutes.

3. Add onion, parsley and tomatoes, stirring frequently.

4. Add okra, and when well-browned, add the juice of the tomatoes, the bay leaf and red pepper. (The okra is very delicate and liable to scorch if not stirred frequently.)

5. When fried and browned, add the boiling water and set on the stove, letting it simmer for about an hour longer. Season with salt and pepper.

6. Serve hot with rice.

Cajun Christmas Creations
Crowley, La.

1 tablespoon of lard

1 chicken, cut into serving pieces

2 large slices of ham, diced

1 onion, chopped

1 sprig of parsley, chopped

6 whole ripe tomatoes, peeled and chopped (Reserve juice)

2 pints of okra, cut into 1/2-inch pieces

1 bay leaf

1/2 pod of red pepper, minced

Salt and cayenne

3 to 4 quarts of boiling water

Chicken & Andouille Gumbo I

8 boneless chicken breast halves

Seasoning Mix (Recipe follows)

1 1/2 cups of all-purpose flour

1 cup of lard

2 cups of chopped onion

1 cup of chopped bellpepper

1 cup of chopped celery

3 quarts of Louisiana Brown Poultry Stock (See recipe, page 38.) or canned chicken broth

1 pound of andouille sausage, cut into bite-sized pieces

1 1/2 teaspoons of minced garlic

Salt

Freshly ground black pepper

Cayenne pepper

2 cups of sliced fresh okra or 1 10-ounce package of frozen okra, thawed

1 cup of sliced green onion

1/2 cup of minced parsley

5 cups of hot cooked rice

Gumbo may be fashioned from almost any ingredient on hand as evidenced by this popular chicken and andouille combination. Andouille is a hearty Cajun sausage somewhat on the spicy side.

1. Remove skin from chicken, if necessary. Cut chicken into bite-sized pieces. Place pieces on a baking sheet; sprinkle liberally with Seasoning Mix (Recipe follows). Let stand at room temperature 30 minutes.

2. Place flour in a plastic bag; add seasoned chicken to coat all pieces thoroughly. Remove chicken; shake in a colander to remove all excess flour, reserving flour.

3. Heat one cup of lard in a large soup pot or Dutch oven over medium-high heat. When very hot, add chicken in batches; stir until browned and crisp on all sides.

4. Remove from heat. Remove chicken with a slotted spoon; set aside.

5. Loosen any browned bits from bottom of pan; strain fat to remove particles. Add enough lard to strained fat to equal one cup. Add fat back to pot over medium-low heat. Add reserved flour; whisk until you have a smooth mahogany-colored roux, for about 45 minutes.

6. Remove roux from heat; add onion, bellpepper and celery at once; stir to blend and prevent browning. Cook until vegetables are wilted and onion is transparent.

7. Slowly stir-in stock; stir until combined before adding more. When all stock has been added, bring to a full boil.

8. Reduce heat; add sausage, garlic, salt, black pepper and cayenne. Add browned chicken; simmer 25 minutes, stirring often.

9. Add okra; cook 20 minutes.

10. To serve, remove from heat; stir-in green onion and parsley. Place a half cup of rice in each soup plate. Spoon gumbo over rice.

Makes 8 to 10 servings.

SEASONING MIX

Prepare seasoning mix by combining all ingredients in a small bowl.

Terry Thompson
Cajun-Creole Cooking

1/2 teaspoon each of salt, freshly ground black pepper, cayenne pepper, paprika, onion powder, and garlic powder

Chicken & Andouille Gumbo II

1 chicken, cut up or boned

1 cup of oil

1 1/2 pounds of andouille sausage, cut into 1-inch slices

1 cup of flour

4 cups of chopped onion

2 cups of chopped celery

2 cups of chopped bellpepper

1 tablespoon of chopped garlic

8 cups of stock or flavored water

All-purpose seasoning

2 cups of chopped green onions

Cooked rice

Filé

1. Season and brown the chicken in the oil over medium-high heat.

2. Add the sausage to the pot and sauté with the chicken. Remove both from the pot.

3. Make a roux with equal parts of oil and flour. The mixture must be free of food particles to avoid burning.

4. Add the onion, celery, bellpepper and later the garlic to the roux, stirring continuously until the vegetables reach the desired tenderness.

5. Return the chicken and sausage to the pot and cook with the vegetables, continuing to stir frequently. Gradually stir-in the liquid and bring to a boil. Reduce the heat and simmer for an hour or more.

6. Season, to taste.

7. Approximately ten minutes before serving, add the green onions.

8. Serve over hot rice. Adding sherry to the gumbo at the table is an option. Place filé on the table, to be added to each bowl of gumbo, at one-fourth to one-half teaspoon, if desired.

Makes 15 servings.

Joe Cahn
The New Orleans School of Cooking
New Orleans, La.

Chicken & Sausage Gumbo

1. Stir flour in oil on medium-high heat to make a roux. Cook until the roux reaches the color of dark coffee.

2. Add chopped onion and celery. Stir for a short period.

3. Add four quarts of water and chicken.

4. Boil one hour, adding salt and pepper, to taste.

5. Add sausage and boil another hour.

6. Skim fat off top.

7. Add onion tops and parsley.

8. Serve over rice in soup plate.

Makes 12 to 14 servings.

Marie L. Broussard
Kaplan, La.

2 cups of flour

1 3/4 cups of oil

1 large onion, chopped

2 stalks of celery, chopped

4 quarts of water

1 large hen, cut into serving pieces
(Don't use a fryer)

3 to 5 pounds of sausage, cut into
2-inch pieces

1 bunch of onion tops, chopped

4 or 5 stalks of parsley, chopped

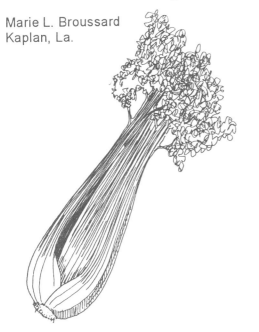

Chicken & Sausage Filé Gumbo

3 pounds of chicken thighs
or drumsticks

1 pound of gizzards

1 cup of oil

1 cup of flour

1 1/2 cups of chopped onion

1/2 cup of chopped celery

1/2 cup of chopped bellpepper

3 quarts of hot water

1 pound of thinly sliced smoked
sausage

Filé

Tabasco sauce, to taste

1. Season chicken pieces and gizzards with salt and pepper.

2. Sear chicken in hot oil. Remove chicken and set aside.

3. Add flour to oil, stirring constantly. Cook flour until dark brown.

4. Add onion, celery and bellpepper; cook until vegetables are transparent.

5. Add hot water and gizzards; return chicken to gumbo and simmer one hour.

6. Add sausage and simmer 30 minutes.

7. Serve over hot rice with pinch of filé and Tabasco.

Bea Weber
Abbeville, La.

Chicken Gumbo
With Smoked Sausage

1. Heat oil on moderate heat. Add flour, stirring constantly. Cook until flour is dark brown.

2. Add hen, stirring to coat with the roux.

3. Add onion, celery and bellpepper. Cook until onion has wilted.

4. Add water and bouillon cubes. Bring to a boil then lower heat to simmer. Simmer one and a half hours.

5. Add sausage; simmer 20 minutes.

6. Add onion tops and parsley.

7. Serve with a dash of Tabasco over hot cooked rice.

Bea Weber
Abbeville, La.

1 cup of oil

1 cup of all-purpose flour

1 large hen, cut up and seasoned with salt and cayenne

3/4 cup of onion, chopped

1/4 cup of celery, chopped

1/4 cup of bellpepper, chopped

4 quarts of water

4 chicken bouillon cubes

1 pound of smoked sausage, cut into 1-inch pieces

Onion tops and parsley, chopped

Tabasco sauce (optional)

Chicken, Sausage & Andouille Gumbo

1 3- to 4-pound hen,
cut into frying pieces

Salt and cayenne pepper

1 cup of oil

1 cup of flour

2 medium onions, chopped

1 medium bellpepper, chopped

2 stalks of celery, chopped

10 cups of chicken stock

2 bay leaves

1 teaspoon of thyme

1 pound of andouille,
cut into 1/2-inch slices

2 dozen oysters

Food writer Marcelle Bienvenu has these thoughts about making gumbo:

I needed a hen. Mama always said that a hen makes a better gumbo. I pulled a package of andouille from the freezer and made a note to pick up some oysters. Let's see... I'll need french bread, and should I get some sweet potatoes or make a "wet" potato salad? You see, there are some Cajuns who just have to have a baked sweet potato floating in their gumbo. Others will tell you that it's a must to put a mound of potato salad in your gumbo. Forget the rice.

Yep, today it was going to be potato salad for me and whatever friends I could round up to come and share in my gumbo. As I ran to my car, I knew it was a perfect day for gumbo. It was cold and windy. There wasn't a leaf left on the trees, and there were dark clouds rolling in from the west. A real gumbo day ahead.

1. Season the chicken well with salt and cayenne pepper.

2. Make a dark roux by slowly browning the oil and flour in a black iron pot or heavy saucepan, stirring constantly.

3. When the roux is about the color of a teddy bear, add the onion, bellpepper and celery and cook until vegetables are wilted, 10 to 15 minutes.

4. Add the chicken stock. (I usually warm it up a bit before adding it to the roux mixture.)

5. Add the chicken. (There are those who will tell you to brown the chicken first, but I throw it in raw.)

6. Add bay leaves and thyme. Cook over medium heat for one hour.

7. Add the andouille and cook for at least another hour. (I like to cook it for a total of three hours, so if you have the time, let it simmer.)

8. Check seasonings. A few minutes before serving, add the oysters and their liquid and cook until the oysters curl. (During the cooking time, if the gumbo becomes too thick, simply add more chicken stock or water.)

9. If you like filé powder, put a dish of it on the table and let people help themselves.

Marcelle Bienvenu
St. Martinville, La.

Chicken, Gizzard & Two-Sausage Gumbo

1 3- to 4-pound hen,
cut into serving pieces

1 pound of gumbo sausage,
cut in 2-inch pieces

1 pound of pork sausage,
cut in 2-inch pieces

1/4 cup of ready-made roux

1 cup of chopped onion

1/4 cup of chopped celery

1/4 cup of chopped bellpepper

1/2 gallon of water

1 pound of chicken gizzards

2 chicken bouillon cubes

3 tablespoons of Season-All

1 tablespoon of salt, or to taste

1/4 cup of chopped green onion

Hot cooked rice

Filé powder

1. Sauté the chicken and sausage together. Set aside. Drain the oil remaining in the pot. Keep two tablespoons of fat in the pan with the meat residue.

2. Add the roux, onion, celery and bellpepper. Fry 10 minutes, stirring constantly.

3. Add a half gallon of cold water to the pot. Bring to a boil for 10 to 15 minutes.

4. Add the gizzards. Cook 20 minutes on a slow boil.

5. Add the chicken; continue cooking 30 minutes. Test the hen to determine if the meat is cooked.

6. Add the sausage and the chicken bouillon cubes. Cook until the chicken is tender.

7. Add Season-All and salt; adjust seasonings, to taste. Add green onion.

8. Serve in gumbo bowls over rice. Offer filé powder and Tabasco at the table.

Note: Serve with potato salad, pickled mirliton (vegetable pear) and hot french bread.

Albert Perrin
Kaplan, La.

Chicken, Oyster & Andouille Gumbo

1. In a heavy pot, heat oil over moderate heat.

2. Gradually add flour, stirring constantly; brown flour until it is dark brown.

3. Add onion and sauté in roux until transparent.

4. Add water, bouillon cubes, Worcestershire sauce, Tabasco, andouille and chicken.

5. Bring to a boil, then lower heat to simmer. Cook one and a half hours or until chicken is done. Taste for seasoning.

6. Add oysters and liquid. Cook until edges of oysters curl.

7. Add onion tops and parsley. Season if needed.

8. Serve over hot cooked rice.

Bea Weber
Abbeville, La.

1 cup of oil

1 cup of flour

1 1/2 cups of chopped onion

4 quarts of water

3 chicken bouillon cubes

1 tablespoon of Worcestershire sauce

1 tablespoon of Tabasco

1 1/2 pounds of andouille, cut into one-inch pieces

1 large hen, cut into serving pieces and seasoned with salt and pepper

2 pints of oysters, with liquid

1 cup of onion tops

1 cup of parsley

Chicken, Sausage & Oyster Gumbo

1 3 1/2-pound fryer,
cut into serving pieces

1/2 teaspoon of salt

1/2 teaspoon of red pepper

3 tablespoons of vegetable oil

1 cup of Basic Roux (See recipe,
page 23.)

1 pound of smoked or Polish
sausage, sliced into 1-inch pieces

3 cloves of garlic, minced

1 cup of finely chopped onion

1 cup of finely chopped bellpepper

2/3 cup of finely chopped celery

1 1/2 quarts of chicken broth,
divided

1/2 teaspoon of salt

1 1/2 teaspoons of freshly ground
pepper

1/4 teaspoon of red pepper

1 teaspoon of dried thyme leaves

The rich taste of this filé gumbo comes from simmering chicken and sausage for a long time. Filé powder is added at the end to slightly thicken and flavor the gumbo.

1. Trim excess fat from chicken. Sprinkle chicken with half a teaspoon of salt and half a teaspoon of red pepper; let stand at room temperature 15 minutes.

2. Heat oil in a very large, heavy pot over medium-high heat; add chicken pieces and brown on all sides. Remove chicken from pot and set aside. Drain oil.

3. Add next six ingredients to pot; cook over low heat, stirring constantly, for 10 minutes.

4. Stir-in a quarter cup of broth and next five ingredients.

5. Add reserved chicken and remaining broth; bring to a boil, stirring gently. Reduce heat and simmer, uncovered, for 45 minutes or until chicken is very tender.

6. Remove chicken pieces from pot then remove skin and bones. Tear chicken into large chunks, then return to pot.

7. Add oysters, green onion tops and parsley; cook four to five minutes or until oysters curl at edges.

8. Remove gumbo from heat, and stir-in filé powder. Let stand five minutes after adding filé, then serve over rice in deep bowls.

Makes four quarts.

Debbie Maugans Barton
"Make-Ahead Roux For
   Quick Cajun Cooking."
Creative Ideas For Living

3 bay leaves, finely crushed

2 (12-ounce) containers of oysters, undrained

1/3 cup of minced green onion tops

1/3 cup of minced fresh parsley

3 tablespoons of filé

Chicken & Oyster Gumbo

1 cup of cooking oil

1 cup of flour

1 large onion, chopped

2 cloves of garlic, minced

1 large hen, cut into serving pieces

2 quarts of warm water

Cayenne pepper, black pepper and salt

1 pint of oysters

Parsley, minced

Onion tops, minced

(This prize-winner is a mellow gumbo—and quick to make.)

1. Make a roux by heating oil and adding flour. Blend well and cook until the flour browns, about five minutes.

2. Add onion and garlic and cook.

3. Season chicken well.

4. Fry chicken in the roux until oil comes out around edges.

5. Add warm water and cook slowly about two hours until chicken is tender.

6. Season with peppers and salt.

7. Add oysters 20 minutes before serving in a large tureen.

8. Sprinkle with minced parsley, onion tops and filé.

9. Serve with rice, french bread and red wine.

Mrs. Lester Montegut
St. Martinville, La.

Chicken & Tasso Gumbo

1. Boil okra in water for about 15 minutes.

2. Lower heat to medium and add tasso and seasonings. Let this cook for about a half hour.

3. Add chicken. Cook at medium for another hour (for fryer) or longer (for hen).

3 cups of smothered okra
(Recipe follows)

6 quarts of water

1/2 pound of tasso, cubed

Red pepper, salt and filé, to taste

1 fryer or hen, cut into serving
pieces

SMOTHERED OKRA

Place all ingredients in a heavy pot that has been lightly oiled. Cook on low heat for at least two hours, stirring often. (Can be frozen until needed for gumbo.)

Catherine Trahan
Kaplan, La.

3 or 4 pounds of fresh or frozen
okra, sliced

3 tomatoes, cut into small pieces

1 large onion, chopped

Salt and pepper, to taste

French Filé Gumbo

2 tablespoons of lard

2 tablespoons of flour

1 large onion, finely chopped

2 cloves of garlic, minced

2 sprigs of parsley, minced

1 bay leaf

Salt and pepper, to taste

2 quarts of water

1/2 hen or 1 fryer, cut into small portions

1 slice of cooked ham, diced

12 freshly shucked oysters with liquid

1 teaspoon of filé

1. Heat lard in soup kettle. Add flour. Cook, stirring, until dark brown.

2. Add onion, garlic, parsley, bay leaf, salt and pepper. Cook until onion is wilted.

3. Add water, chicken and ham. Bring to boil; cover, simmer for one and a half hours, or until chicken is tender, adding water if needed.

4. Add oysters. Cook for 15 minutes longer.

5. Remove from heat. Stir-in filé before serving.

Serves six.

Mrs. George C. Poret
The General Federation
of Women's Clubs Cookbook:
America Cooks

Crockery Chicken Gumbo

1. Place chicken, okra, onions, carrots, garlic, sprigs of parsley, thyme, rice and water into crock pot.

2. Cook 10 to 12 hours on low.

3. Remove chicken; discard bones and cut meat into small pieces. Return meat to crock pot.

4. Taste for seasoning; add green onions and parsley. Add salt and pepper if needed.

5. Serve with Tabasco.

Bea Weber
Abbeville, La.

3 pounds of chicken, cut up and seasoned with salt and black pepper

1 10-ounce package of frozen cut okra

2 medium onions, cut into chunks

2 medium carrots, scraped and cut into 1-inch pieces

2 medium cloves of garlic, peeled

3 sprigs of fresh parsley

1/2 teaspoon of thyme

1 cup of raw rice

9 cups of water

1 cup of chopped green onions

1/2 cup of parsley, chopped

Tabasco sauce

Chicken & Shrimp Gumbo

1 fryer or hen,
cut into serving pieces

Salt

Black pepper and red pepper

1 cup of fat

3/4 cup of flour

1 cup of chopped onion

2 pounds of shrimp, cleaned

1 clove of garlic

1/2 cup of celery

1/2 cup of parsley

1/2 cup of green onion tops

1. Season chicken with salt and pepper; brown in fat in heavy iron skillet.

2. As the pieces are browned, place chicken in an iron pot large enough to hold four quarts of water along with other ingredients.

3. Make a roux by adding flour to hot fat in which meat was browned. (Stir constantly, keeping heat low until flour is a reddish-golden brown. Be sure that the fat glistens above the flour before adding additional ingredients or the roux will be pasty.)

4. Add chopped onion and stir until it becomes transparent.

5. Add roux to large kettle of chicken; stir-in one quart of water. Lower heat, cover pot and let simmer, stirring often to prevent sticking, adding more water as necessary.

6. When chicken begins to get tender, add four quarts of water, shrimp and remaining ingredients.

7. Season, to taste. Let cook about 45 minutes longer.

8. Serve with rice. Add to each bowl of gumbo about one demitasse spoon of filé.

Miss Gertrude Hebert
Olivier, La.

Chicken-Crawfish Gumbo

1. Season chicken with Accent, salt and cayenne pepper, then set aside.

2. Heat oil in skillet to medium heat. Brown chicken until light brown. Remove chicken.

3. Add flour; cook until light brown, stirring frequently.

4. Stir-in onion, celery, bellpepper and garlic. Cook slowly, until roux is deep brown and onion is transparent.

5. In an eight-quart Dutch oven or gumbo pot, combine hot water, roux and chicken pieces. Cook slowly for about 45 minutes.

6. Add thawed crawfish tails, onion tops and parsley; cook an additional 30 minutes.

7. Serve with hot cooked rice.

Serves six.

Mrs. Virgie B. Foreman
Rayne, La.

1 fryer, cut into serving pieces

1 1/2 teaspoons of monosodium glutamate (Accent)

1 teaspoon of salt

1/8 teaspoon of cayenne pepper

1/2 cup of oil

1/2 cup of flour

1 cup of chopped onion

1/2 cup of chopped celery

1/2 cup of chopped bellpepper

3 cloves of garlic, minced

9 cups of hot water

1 pound of cleaned, frozen crawfish tails, thawed or fresh crawfish tails

1/4 cup of chopped green onion tops

1/4 cup of snipped parsley

Chicken & Lobster Gumbo

1 cup of oil

1 cup of flour

1 large hen, cut into pieces and seasoned with salt and pepper

2 cups of chopped onion

1/2 cup of chopped celery

1/2 cup of chopped bellpepper

1 quart of cold water

2 bottles of clam juice

3 quarts of boiling water

3 tablespoons of Worcestershire sauce

5 tablespoons of Tabasco sauce

2 or more cans of lobster

1. Heat oil on moderate heat; add flour, stirring constantly until flour is dark brown.

2. Add hen to roux. Stir for 10 minutes.

3. Add onion, celery and bellpepper; sauté until vegetables are wilted.

4. Add one quart of cold water. Bring mixture to a boil.

5. Add clam juice and boiling water. Boil until chicken is almost tender, about two and a half hours.

6. Add Worcestershire sauce, Tabasco and lobster.

7. Cook a few minutes.

8. Remove from heat.

9. Serve over hot cooked rice. You may add one pinch of filé per serving, if desired.

Bea Weber
Abbeville, La.

Chicken, Ham & Seafood Gumbo

1. In a heavy pot, brown flour in oil, stirring constantly, until flour is dark brown.

2. Add onion and bellpepper; sauté until onion is wilted.

3. Add hen and ham; coat with roux.

4. Add water and clam juice.

5. Bring to a boil, then simmer for one hour or until chicken is almost done.

6. Add shrimp and catfish. Cook 20 minutes.

7. Add oysters and liquid. Cook until oysters curl.

8. Turn heat off. Add onion tops and parsley.

9. Serve over hot cooked rice.

Bea Weber
Abbeville, La.

---

1 cup of all-purpose flour

1 cup of oil

1 cup of chopped onion

1/4 cup of chopped bellpepper

1 large hen, cut up and seasoned with salt and pepper

1 cup of ham, cut into cubes

4 quarts of water

2 bottles of clam juice

1 pound of raw, peeled shrimp, seasoned with salt and red pepper

1 1/2 pounds of catfish nuggets, seasoned with salt and red pepper

1 pint of oysters with liquid

3/4 cup each of onion tops and parsley, chopped

Hen & Sausage Gumbo

Salt, black pepper & cayenne pepper, to taste

1 teaspoon of paprika

1/2 cup of all-purpose flour

1 4-pound hen, cut into pieces, rinsed and patted dry

1/2 cup of vegetable oil

2 medium onions, chopped

1 bunch of green onions, diced

3 cloves of garlic, minced

1 (10-ounce) can of Rotel tomatoes, chopped

1 teaspoon of thyme

4 quarts of water

1 quart of canned chicken broth

1 1/2 pounds of andouille sausage, cut into 1/2-inch slices

1 bay leaf

1 teaspoon of Worcestershire sauce

1 (8-ounce) bottle of clam juice

20 ounces of frozen okra

1/2 cup of chopped parsley

1. In a bowl, combine the cayenne, salt, black pepper, paprika and flour. Dredge the hen pieces in seasoned flour. Reserve remaining flour for use in Step 4, below.

2. In a heavy pot, heat the vegetable oil on medium to high heat. Cook the hen until golden brown. Place the cooked hen on a bed of paper towels to absorb any excess oil.

3. Using the oil and hen residue at the bottom of the pot, sauté the onions, green onions, garlic and Rotel tomatoes, stirring occasionally, for five minutes.

4. Add the leftover seasoned flour and the thyme; cook for five minutes, stirring constantly.

5. Add the water, chicken broth, andouille sausage, bay leaf, Worcestershire sauce and the clam juice. Bring to a boil. The mixture should be stirred occasionally.

6. Add the hen and simmer for 45 minutes.

7. Once the hen is tender, remove it from the pot. Allow it to cool; then debone the meat and cut it into bite-size pieces. Place the hen pieces in the gumbo.

8. Add the okra, parsley and

bellpepper. Remove the bay leaf and discard it. Cook for five additional minutes.

9. Adjust the seasonings. Add Tabasco sauce, to taste.

10. To serve, mound rice in pre-heated gumbo bowls; ladle gumbo over the rice and garnish with parsley and green onion tops.

11. Offer filé to guests at table.

12. Be sure guests receive pieces of hen and sausage in each serving.

Bea Weber
Abbeville, La.

1/2 cup of chopped bellpepper

6 drops of Tabasco sauce

Hot cooked rice

Green onion tops, chopped fine

Filé

Hen Combination Seafood Gumbo

1/2 cup of cooking oil

4 tablespoons of flour

1 cup of chopped onion

1 cup of chopped celery

1 cup of chopped bellpepper

1 clove of garlic

1 hen, cut into serving pieces

Salt

Pepper

10 1/2 cups of warm water

3 pounds of sausage,
cut into one-inch slices

3 cups of raw shrimp, deveined
and peeled

1 dozen oysters

1. Sauté onion, celery, bellpepper and garlic in hot oil with flour about six minutes or until golden brown.

2. Season hen with salt and pepper. Put hen in pot, then add water.

3. Cook on low for two hours.

4. Add the sausage, shrimp and oysters and cook for 20 to 30 minutes more.

Serves five.

Emelda Citizen
Lafayette, La.

FOWL & WILD GAME

Duck Gumbo

4 slices of bacon, fried and diced

1 cup of chopped onion

1/4 cup of flour

2 quarts of boiling water

1/4 teaspoon of salt

1/4 teaspoon of ground black pepper

1 duck (3½ to 4 pounds), or 2 wild ducks, cut up

2 cups of shelled and deveined shrimp

2 cups of cooked tomatoes

1 cup of chopped green onion

1 cup of chopped parsley

2 tablespoons of filé

1 pint of shucked oysters

6 cups of cooked rice

1. Sauté onion in bacon fat with bacon until light brown.

2. Stir-in flour, then boiling water, salt and pepper. Stir well.

3. Add duck to kettle. Add more water to cover, if necessary.

4. Cover and simmer for one and a half hours.

5. Cool; skim fat from top. Add shrimp and tomatoes and cook 20 minutes more.

6. Remove from heat and add green onion tops, parsley, filé and oysters.

7. Serve over rice.

Makes 8 to 10 servings.

USA Rice Council

Fernand Dubois Wild Duck Gumbo

1. Season ducks with salt, pepper and Tabasco.

2. Melt shortening in heavy iron pot. Add flour, stirring constantly to make a very dark roux.

3. Add onion and cook until transparent.

4. Add duck pieces and cook until brown.

5. Add water, green onions, garlic, parsley and seasonings.

6. Simmer about two hours or until duck is tender.

Serves six.

"Cajun-Creole Cookery"
The Daily Iberian
New Iberia, La.

2 wild ducks, cut into serving pieces

1/2 cup of shortening

1/2 cup of flour

1 cup of chopped onion

2 quarts of water

1/4 cup of green onions

2 cloves of garlic, chopped

1/2 cup of chopped parsley

Salt, black pepper and Tabasco, to taste

Wild Duck & Okra Gumbo

1 wild duck, cut into serving pieces

1/3 cup of fat

8 cups of okra, chopped fine

2 onions, chopped

8 cloves of garlic, chopped

7 cups of water

3 large tomatoes, chopped

Salt, black pepper and red pepper

1. Brown duck or other poultry in hot fat.

2. Remove meat and pour fat into aluminum pot. (Iron pot will turn okra black).

3. Cook okra in fat with onion and garlic. Cook slowly, stirring frequently until okra is no longer gummy.

4. Return duck to okra and add seven cups of water.

5. Add tomatoes and season with salt, black pepper and red pepper. Cook 30 to 45 minutes.

6. Serve with filé and hot cooked rice.

"Cajun-Creole Cookery"
The Daily Iberian
New Iberia, La.

Wild Duck & Oyster Gumbo

1. Melt shortening. When hot, add flour to make a roux. When roux is browned, add onion. Cook until tender.

2. Season duck with salt and pepper.

3. When onions are tender in roux, add the duck pieces. Let fry in the roux until blood in duck disappears.

4. Add water. Let boil slowly until duck is very tender.

5. Add oyster liquid and oysters. Cook about ten minutes longer.

6. Season again if necessary after oysters have been added.

Mrs. Elton Beaullieu
Jeanerette, La.

1 heaping tablespoon of shortening

2 heaping tablespoons of flour

1 large or 2 small onions, chopped

1 wild duck, cut into six pieces

Salt and pepper

2 quarts of water

2 dozen oysters and liquid

Duck, Oyster & Sausage Gumbo

2 large wild ducks, cleaned

2 stalks of celery with leaves, cut into 2-inch pieces

1 medium onion, sliced

1 tablespoon of salt

Chicken broth

1 pound of hot smoked sausage, cut into 1-inch pieces

1/2 cup of vegetable oil

1/2 cup of all-purpose flour

3/4 cup of finely chopped celery

1 cup of chopped onion

1 bellpepper, finely chopped

Salt and pepper, to taste

6 green onions with tops, finely chopped

2 tablespoons of chopped fresh parsley

1 pint of oysters, undrained

Hot cooked rice

Gumbo filé

1. Combine first four ingredients in a large Dutch oven; cover with water and bring to a boil.

2. Reduce heat; cover and simmer about one hour or until ducks are tender.

3. Remove ducks from stock; reserve stock. When ducks cool, remove meat from bones; cut meat into bite-size pieces and set aside.

4. Return skin and bones to stock; cover and simmer an additional hour.

5. Strain stock; add enough chicken broth to make two and a half quarts of liquid. Set aside.

6. Cook sausage over medium heat about five minutes, stirring occasionally. Drain on paper towels and set aside.

7. Heat oil in a five-quart heavy iron pot or Dutch oven; stir-in flour. Cook over medium heat at least 30 minutes or until a dark roux is formed, stirring constantly.

8. Add celery, onion and bellpepper; cook over medium heat 10 minutes, stirring constantly.

9. Remove from heat, and gradually stir-in reserved hot stock. Bring mixture to a boil; then

reduce heat and simmer 20 minutes.

10. Add duck, sausage, salt and pepper to stock mixture; simmer 20 minutes.

11. Stir-in green onion and parsley; simmer 20 minutes.

12. Add oysters; simmer an additional 10 minutes.

13. Serve gumbo over hot cooked rice. Thicken each serving with gumbo filé.

Makes 8 to 10 servings.

Note: Gumbo is best when made a day ahead, refrigerated and reheated.

"Cajun Creole Cookery"
The Daily Iberian

Duck & Sausage Gumbo

1 pound of hot sausage, skinned and sliced

Vegetable oil

2 five-pound ducks, cut into serving pieces

4 teaspoons of salt

Freshly ground black pepper

1/2 cup of flour

6 tablespoons of brown roux

1 cup of finely chopped onion

1/2 cup of finely chopped green onions

1 cup of finely chopped celery

1 cup of finely chopped bellpeppers

3 quarts of warm water

1/2 teaspoon of Tabasco

1 1/2 teaspoons of ground hot red pepper

1/4 cup of finely chopped fresh parsley

2 teaspoons of filé

6 to 8 cups of freshly cooked long-grain rice

1. In a heavy, ungreased 12-inch skillet, fry the sausage over low heat, turning the slices frequently with a slotted spatula until the bottom of the pan is filled with fat.

2. Increase the heat to moderate and, turning the slices occasionally, continue to fry until the sausage is richly browned.

3. Transfer the sausage slices to paper towels to drain. There should be about a half cup of fat in the skillet; if not, add vegetable oil to make up that amount.

4. Season the birds with two teaspoons of the salt and a few grindings of black pepper. Roll the ducks in the flour to coat the pieces on all sides, then vigorously shake off the excess flour.

5. Brown the ducks, five or six pieces at a time, in the hot fat remaining in the skillet. Turn the pieces frequently with tongs and regulate the heat so that they color deeply and evenly without burning. As they brown, transfer the pieces of duck to paper towels to drain.

6. Warm the roux over low heat in a heavy 12-quart enameled or cast iron pot.

7. When the roux is smooth and fluid, stir-in the onions, green onions and celery. Stirring frequently, cook over moderate heat for about five minutes, or until the vegetables are soft. Mix-in the bellpeppers.

8.   Stirring constantly, pour-in the warm water in a slow, thin stream and bring to a boil over high heat.

9. Add the sausage slices, the pieces of duck, the remaining two teaspoons of salt, the Tabasco and the red pepper.

10. When the mixture returns to a boil, reduce the heat to low and cover the pot partially. Simmer the gumbo for two hours.

11. Remove the pot from the heat and, with a large spoon, skim as much fat from the surface as possible. Stir-in the parsley and filé, then taste for seasoning. (The gumbo should be hotly spiced and may require more Tabasco and/or red pepper.)

12. Ladle the gumbo into a heated tureen and serve at once, accompanied by rice.

Serves six to eight.

Cajun Christmas Creations

Duck & Artichoke Gumbo

1 cup of Cajun Roux
(See recipe, page 24)

1/4 cup of chopped green onions

1 large onion, chopped

3 celery stalks, chopped

1 medium carrot, chopped

1 medium bellpepper, chopped

4 quarts of Duck Stock
(Recipe follows)

Meat of 2 or 3 ducks
(Recipe follows)

1 1/2 14-ounce cans of artichoke
hearts, drained and quartered

2 bay leaves, minced

2 teaspoons of dried leaf chervil
or 2 tablespoons of chopped fresh
chervil

1/8 teaspoon of ground cloves

1/4 teaspoon of cayenne

This rich and hearty gumbo is a must for the duck lover. Even the roux is made with duck fat! It is served over wild rice for a perfect combination of flavors. For easy preparation, make stock and roux one day, refrigerate overnight, and prepare gumbo the next day.

1. Make roux as directed, using duck fat and enough lard to make one cup. Cook roux until mahogany-colored.

2. Add green onions, onion, celery, carrot and bellpepper to hot roux. Cook, stirring until vegetables are wilted and transparent, about 10 minutes.

3. Meanwhile, bring reserved four quarts of Duck Stock to a rapid boil in an eight-quart soup pot. Add reserved duck meat and artichoke hearts.

4. Slowly stir roux mixture into boiling stock, one large spoonful at a time.

5. Reduce heat. Add seasonings; simmer for one hour.

6. Stir-in vermouth; heat through.

7. Taste for seasoning; adjust if necessary.

8. Spoon about a half cup of rice into each soup plate; spoon gumbo over rice. Sprinkle with parsley and green onions.

Makes 8 to 10 servings

1 teaspoon of freshly ground black pepper

Salt, to taste

1 cup of dry vermouth

5 cups of hot cooked wild rice

Minced parsley, preferably flat-leaf

Chopped green onions

DUCK STOCK

1. Preheat oven to 400 degrees.

2. Pull fat from inside of ducks; reserve.

3. Quarter ducks; place pieces in two roasting pans. Roast in preheated oven until ducks are brown in color, one to one and a half hours. Turn pieces often.

4. Place browned duck in a 10-quart stockpot; set aside.

5. Carefully pour fat from roasting pans into a two-cup Pyrex measuring cup; set aside.

6. Spread vegetables in roasting pans. Bake in preheated oven until vegetables are dark brown, about 30 minutes. Add browned vegetables to stockpot with duck.

2 3- to 4-pound domestic ducks or 3 wild ducks

2 large onions, coarsely chopped

4 celery stalks, chopped

3 leeks, coarsely chopped

2 large carrots, chopped

5 parsley sprigs, preferably flat-leaf

2 teaspoons of dried leaf thyme or 2 tablespoons of chopped fresh thyme

1 tablespoon of peppercorns

2 bay leaves

7. Place roasting pan over high heat; add one cup of water. Using a metal spatula, scrape up all browned bits; add liquid to stockpot. Repeat with second pan.

8. Add enough cold water to cover duck pieces and vegetables by four inches.

9. Bring stock to a full boil; skim gray foam from surface. Reduce heat; stir-in parsley, thyme, peppercorns and bay leaf.

10. Barely simmer, uncovered, for six hours. Strain stock through a fine strainer, pressing down on meat and vegetables to extract every drop of flavor.

11. Discard vegetables; cool duck. Reserve four quarts of stock for gumbo. Freeze any extra for another use.

12. As soon as duck pieces are cool enough to handle, pull the meat from the bones and chop it into bite-sized pieces for gumbo. Reserve meat. Discard skin and bones.

Terry Thompson
Cajun-Creole Cooking

Duck Hunter's Camp Gumbo

This innocent-looking gumbo is not for beginners. Despite its simple list of ingredients, it comes from that domain of south Louisiana males—the hunting camp— where recipes emerge from the ingredients on hand and are never exactly the same the next time around. If you know a hunter who cooks, ask his opinion of your finished gumbo, and don't be afraid to add your own personal touch.

1 cup of flour

1 cup of oil

5 cups of chopped duck gizzards

Salt and pepper

Tabasco sauce

Duck livers, to taste

2 bay leaves

A pinch of rosemary and celery salt

1. Make a roux with the flour and oil and add a pint of hot water.

2. Add the gizzards, salt, pepper and a dash of Tabasco.

3. Slowly add another pint of hot water and cook for 40 minutes or until gizzards are done.

4. Add the duck livers, bay leaves, rosemary and celery salt. Add more hot water and simmer 30 minutes until livers are done.

5. Serve in a bowl with cooked rice and filé. Best with hot french bread and red wine.

Serves four to six.

Mary Land's Louisiana Cookery

Wild Goose Gumbo With Oysters

1/2 cup of all-purpose flour

Salt, black pepper and cayenne pepper, to taste

1 wild goose, cut in pieces

1 pound of goose gizzards

3 tablespoons of bacon drippings or vegetable oil

2 pounds of sliced okra

1 tablespoon of flour

1/2 cup of chopped celery

4 cloves of garlic, finely chopped

1 cup of chopped onion

1/4 cup of bellpepper

1 cup of green onion tops, sliced

1/2 cup of parsley

3 quarts of water

2 bay leaves

1 can of Italian tomato paste

1 tablespoon of Worcestershire

1 tablespoon of French's mustard

1. In a bowl, combine the flour, salt, black pepper, and cayenne pepper. Dredge the goose and gizzards in the seasoned flour. Reserve the dredging flour.

2. In a Dutch oven, heat three tablespoons of bacon drippings over medium-high heat until it is hot. Add the goose and gizzards; cook three minutes per side. Set the cooked pieces on paper towels to drain.

3. Sauté sliced okra until the okra is crisp. Cook the okra until it has ceased to be stringy. Add one tablespoon of flour, stirring occasionally. Add the celery, garlic, onion, and bellpepper. Cook until onion begins to brown, about five minutes.

4. Add the reserved dredging flour and cook three minutes.

5. Add the green onion tops, parsley, water, bay leaves, tomato paste, Worcestershire, mustard, chicken broth and bouillon cubes. Increase the heat to medium-high and bring to a boil, stirring frequently.

6. Add the goose and gizzards, reduce the heat to medium, cover, and simmer for 45 minutes.

7. Remove the goose and gizzards. Allow the meat to cool. Remove the meat from the bones. Cut the goose meat and gizzards into cubes and return it to the gumbo.

8. Add the oysters, their liquid, and Tabasco. Cook until the edges of the oysters curl. (This should take just a few minutes.)

9. Adjust the seasoning to taste. Remove the bay leaves and discard.

10. To serve, mound rice in gumbo bowls, ladle some gumbo over the rice, and garnish with parsley and green onion tops.

11. Be sure each guest receives goose, gizzard and oysters in each serving.

Bea Weber
Abbeville, La.

1 quart of chicken broth

3 chicken bouillon cubes

3 dozen oysters and liquid

6 drops of Tabasco sauce

Hot cooked rice

Wild Goose Gumbo

2 tablespoons of shortening

2 pounds of okra, sliced

1 tablespoon of flour

1/2 cup of chopped celery

2 cloves of garlic, minced

1 onion, chopped

1 bellpepper, chopped

2 quarts of water

2 bay leaves

2 tablespoons of salt

1 can of tomato paste

1 wild goose, cut into serving pieces

1. Heat the shortening in a large soup kettle and sauté the okra until it is crisp and no longer stringy or runny.

2. Stir-in flour and add celery, garlic, onion and bellpepper. Cook, stirring, until the onion is transparent.

3. Add water, bay leaves, salt and tomato paste.

4. Bring the mixture to a boil, lower the heat and simmer the gumbo for two and a half hours.

5. In the meantime, simmer the goose in salted water to cover until the bird is tender. Cut the goose meat from the bones, dice it and add it to the gumbo. Simmer 10 minutes longer.

Gourmet Magazine

Turkey Gumbo

1. Make a stock by boiling the turkey carcass in three quarts of water seasoned with a small amount of salt and pepper, the quartered onion, the stalk of celery and the poultry seasoning.

2. Boil carcass until meat falls off; strain stock and discard the vegetables. Reserve the pieces of turkey meat and the stock.

3. Sauté onion, celery, garlic and bellpepper in butter or bacon grease for about 10 minutes.

4. Add tomatoes, okra, ham, shrimp and seasonings and cook until shrimp turn pink. Add browned flour. Stir frequently to prevent sticking; let this simmer about 10 minutes then add stock, tomato liquid and enough water to fill a one and a half gallon pot.

5. Add the turkey meat. Let simmer one hour.

6. Add parsley. If not thick enough, add more flour.

7. About five minutes before serving, let gumbo come to a rolling boil and add filé. If oysters are used, add them at the same time. Remove pieces of bellpepper.

8. Serve in soup bowls over cooked rice.

Mrs. G.W. Griffin
Cataline Hotel
Pass Christian, Miss.

1 turkey carcass

1 onion, quartered

1 stalk of celery, cut into large pieces

1/2 teaspoon of poultry seasoning

2 onions, chopped

2 cups of chopped celery

2 cloves of garlic, minced

1 large bellpepper, cut in half

3 tablespoons of butter or bacon grease

1 No. 2 can of tomatoes, drained (Reserve the liquid)

1/2 pound of okra, cut in small pieces

1 slice of ham, cut in cubes, or 4 or 5 slices of bacon, cooked and cut in small pieces

1 pound of raw shrimp

Salt, pepper and Tabasco, to taste

Heavy pinch of thyme

1/2 cup of flour, browned in frying pan without oil

1 tablespoon of parsley, chopped

2 tablespoons of filé

2 dozen raw oysters (optional)

Turkey Filé Gumbo

Turkey carcass plus 2 drumsticks

3 tablespoons of oil

3 tablespoons of flour

2 ribs of celery, chopped

1 onion, chopped

1/2 bellpepper, chopped

1 link of smoked sausage, sliced (boil grease out of cut sausage and drain before adding to the gumbo)

2 bay leaves

Salt and pepper, to taste

1/2 pound of raw shrimp, peeled and deveined

1/4 cup of chopped parsley

1. Boil turkey in three quarts of water; remove and debone. Reserve water.

2. Make a roux with oil and flour; cook to golden color.

3. Add celery, onion and bellpepper.

4. Add sausage, water left from turkey and bay leaves. Season, to taste. Simmer about 30 minutes.

5. Add turkey meat, shrimp and parsley. Simmer about 15 minutes.

6. Adjust seasoning. Serve over spoonful of rice in soup bowl. Sprinkle about a half of a teaspoon of filé over top if desired. (Do not cook filé in gumbo.)

Note: One large fryer can be substituted for turkey. If fresh chicken is used, it must be cut in serving portions and fried slightly in shortening. Remove chicken and stir flour into shortening in which chicken was fried, thereby making the golden roux. Two dozen oysters may be added 10 minutes before serving.

Louisiana Recipes from West Baton Rouge Historical Association

Turkey-Oyster Gumbo

Some of my Southern friends look forward to the Thanksgiving and Christmas holiday dinners more for the leftover turkey than the principal menu. Why? Because this means Turkey-Oyster Gumbo. This version is a hardy soup and should be eaten as the main course with crusty french bread.

1. Remove turkey from bones and save.

2. Cook flour in butter to make a dark roux, about 10 minutes.

3. Add onion and sauté for five minutes.

4. Add green onions, stock, water, celery, bay leaves, parsley, thyme, salt and pepper.

5. Add turkey bones. Simmer 45 minutes.

6. Remove bones and discard. Add turkey meat and ham.

7. Simmer 30 minutes.

8. Add oysters and their liquid. Simmer 15 minutes.

9. Remove from heat. Add filé, to taste, 10 minutes before serving.

10. Serve over cooked rice.

Chef Earl Peyroux
Gourmet Cooking By Earl Peyroux

3 cups of turkey meat

Turkey bones

3 tablespoons of butter

2 tablespoons of flour

1 large onion, chopped

10 green onions, chopped

4 cups of chicken stock

2 cups of water

1 1/2 cups of chopped celery

2 bay leaves

1/2 cup of chopped parsley

1/2 teaspoon of thyme

Salt and pepper

1 cup of ham, cubed

2 pints of oysters, undrained

2 tablespoons of filé

Turkey & Sausage Gumbo

Leftover turkey carcass

1/2 cup of oil

1/2 cup of flour

1 cup of chopped onion

1 clove of garlic, finely chopped

1 pound of smoked sausage, cut into one-inch pieces

Salt and pepper, to taste

Chopped onion tops and parsley

1. Remove meat from turkey bones. Simmer bones and meat in one gallon of water for about one hour.

2. Make roux with oil and flour; cook until golden brown.

3. Add chopped onion and garlic and cook until wilted.

4. Add water from simmered turkey bones.

5. Brown sausage on both sides.

6. Add sausage and turkey meat to roux mixture. Continue cooking until meat is tender.

7. Season, to taste. Add onion tops and parsley. Add filé to each plate of gumbo.

"Cajun Creole Cookery"
The Daily Iberian

Smoked Turkey & Sausage Gumbo

This recipe can be adapted to various meats and seafoods.

1. Make a roux by browning the flour in well-heated vegetable oil. Stir continually over low heat until roux is nearly chocolate brown.

2. Add water slowly followed by the turkey. (Leftover turkey bones may be added at this point and removed before serving.)

3. Brown the sausage, remove from skillet and drain. Add to gumbo.

4. Sauté the onion, celery, shallots, bellpepper and parsley in the sausage fat. When tender, add to gumbo.

5. Simmer for several hours. Season to taste with any or all of the listed seasonings.

Bobby Potts
Louisiana and Mississippi Plantation Cookbook

1/2 cup of flour

1/2 cup of oil

3 to 4 quarts of water or chicken stock

1 smoked turkey breast, cut into chunks

2 pounds of smoked sausage, cut into 1/2-inch pieces

3 cups of chopped onion

1 cup of chopped celery

1 cup of chopped shallots

1 cup of chopped bellpepper

1 bunch of parsley, chopped

Thyme

Sage

Cayenne or black pepper

Salt

Tabasco sauce

Worcestershire

Pinch of powdered cloves

Garlic

Mushrooms

Basil

Bird, Sausage & Oyster Gumbo

1 cup of cooking oil

1 cup of flour

1 pound of smoked sausage, cut into 1-inch pieces

1 large onion, sliced thin

8 to 10 birds, dressed and seasoned

1/2 cup each of minced green onions, parsley and celery leaves

1 pod of garlic, minced

1 quart of oysters

Salt and pepper, to taste

Filé

Blackbirds are a common sight wheeling and dipping over rice fields in south Louisiana. A generation ago the birds were a common ingredient in gumbos, and are still found in gumbo pots today, but mostly in rural areas. Dove or quail may be substituted.

1. Make roux by heating oil and blending-in flour until flour browns and oil rises to surface. This requires constant stirring over medium heat. Roux must not scorch.

2. Par-boil sausage in water for 10 minutes to remove some of the fat.

3. Add onion to roux and cook until transparent. Place seasoned birds in roux mixture; add the sausage. Keep stirring until birds are well-seared; add about one quart of warm water and let simmer until tender, about two hours.

4. Add enough hot water to serve eight to ten.

5. Add green onions, parsley, celery leaves, garlic and oysters. Let simmer 10 minutes longer.

6. Season, to taste. Heat soup bowls; add about a half teaspoon of filé to each serving. Serve with steamed fluffy rice.

Serves eight to ten.

Note: As an accompaniment, a green salad, or coleslaw, and french bread make a complete meal. Serve with red wine.

"Cajun Creole Cookery"
The Daily Iberian

Guinea Gumbo

3/4 cup of shortening

3/4 cup of flour

1 onion, chopped

1 guinea, cut into serving pieces

1 1/2 pounds of pork sausage, cut in 2-inch pieces

1/2 cup of chopped onion tops

1/2 cup of chopped parsley

1/2 teaspoon of gumbo filé

1. Heat shortening and add flour, stirring until flour has darkened, to make roux.

2. Add onion and guinea pieces.

3. Add six cups of cold water and mix; bring to a boil and cook until meat is tender.

4. Season, to taste.

5. Put sausage into gumbo a half hour before ready to serve. Add onion tops and parsley 10 minutes before serving.

6. When ready to serve, add filé to each plate.

"Cajun-Creole Cookery"
The Daily Iberian

Squirrel Gumbo

1. Put roux in deep gumbo pot and add the water.

2. Set on medium heat and stir until roux is blended with the water.

3. Add chopped onion, squirrel, salt and red pepper.

4. Cook for a half hour, then add the sausage. Cook for an hour, or until meat tests tender.

5. If done, add onion tops and parsley and cook for 15 minutes more.

6. Taste for seasoning and add more, if necessary.

Roux (Recipe follows)

3 quarts of cold tap water

1 onion, chopped

4 or 5 small squirrels, cut into serving pieces

Salt and red pepper, to taste

1 pound of smoked sausage, cut in bite-size pieces

1/4 cup of chopped green onion tops

1/4 cup of chopped parsley (fresh)

ROUX:

1. Put the oil in an iron pot and heat until warm.

2. Stir-in the flour and cook, stirring constantly, over medium heat until mixture is a pretty caramel brown. (Be sure to scrape bottom often to keep roux from burning.)

3. Remove from heat and set aside.

3 or 4 tablespoons of corn oil

7 or 8 tablespoons of flour

Rena Dupre
Quelque Chose Beaucoup Bon

109

Squirrel Or Rabbit Gumbo

1 fine squirrel or rabbit,
cut into serving pieces

Salt and black pepper

2 tablespoons of butter
or 1 tablespoon of shortening

2 slices or 1/2 pound
of lean ham, diced

1 large onion, chopped

3 sprigs of parsley, finely chopped

1 sprig of thyme, finely chopped

2 quarts of oyster water or plain
boiling water

1 bay leaf, chopped fine

1/2 pod of red pepper, without the
seeds, cut in half

3 dozen raw oysters

2 or 3 tablespoons of filé

This Creole gumbo is reprinted from The Picayune Original Creole Cookbook, *which many consider to be the definitive book on Creole cooking.*

1. Dredge the squirrel or rabbit well with salt and black pepper.

2. Put the shortening or butter into a deep stew pot and when hot, add the squirrel or rabbit and the ham. Cover closely and fry for eight to 10 minutes.

3. Add the onion, parsley and thyme, stirring occasionally to prevent burning. When nicely browned, add the boiling water or the oyster water, which has been thoroughly heated.

4. Add the bay leaf and the pepper pod and set the gumbo back to simmer for about an hour longer.

5. When nearly ready to serve dinner, and while the gumbo is boiling, add the fresh oysters. Let the gumbo remain on the stove for about three minutes longer, and then remove the pot from the fire.

6. Gradually drop the filé into the hot gumbo, stirring slowly to mix thoroughly.

7. Serve with cooked rice, about two tablespoons to one plate of gumbo.

Serves six.

Note: Never boil the gumbo with the rice, and never add the filé while the gumbo is on the fire, as boiling after the filé is added tends to make the gumbo stringy and unfit for use; or else the filé is precipitated to the bottom of the pot, which is equally to be avoided.

The Times-Picayune
The Picayune Original Creole Cookbook

SEAFOOD

Seafood Gumbo I

1 cup of chopped onion

1/2 cup of chopped bellpepper

1/2 cup of chopped celery

2 gallons of shrimp stock

1 1/2 cups of roux

Salt, cayenne pepper and garlic, to taste

1 pound of medium shrimp, peeled

1 pound of claw crabmeat

1 pint of oysters with juice

1. Combine all ingredients except seafood in a large pot and boil on medium heat until the roux is dissolved.

2. Lower heat to a simmer for an additional hour and a half with the pot covered, allowing some steam to escape.

3. For the final minutes of cooking, bring the mixture to a heavy boil, add the seafood ingredients and cook for three minutes, until the shrimp are pink.

Don's Seafood Hut
Lafayette, La.

Seafood Gumbo II

1. Make a roux with equal parts of oil and flour to desired color (brown to dark brown). The mixture must be free of food particles to avoid burning.

2. Add onion, celery, bellpepper, and later the garlic to the roux, and stir continuously until vegetables reach the desired tenderness.

3. Gradually stir-in the liquid and bring to a boil.

4. Add the crabs and simmer for an hour or more.

5. Season, to taste.

6. Approximately ten minutes before serving, add green onions, shrimp, and sautéed okra.

7. Serve over hot cooked rice. Adding sherry at the table is an option. Filé may be placed on the table for guests to add to their gumbo if desired.

Makes 15 servings.

Joe Cahn
The New Orleans School of Cooking
New Orleans, La.

1 cup of oil

1 cup of flour

4 cups of chopped onion

2 cups of chopped celery

2 cups of chopped bellpepper

1 tablespoon of chopped garlic

8 cups of seafood stock

6 crabs, cleaned and quartered

Salt

Cayenne pepper

1 bay leaf

1/2 teaspoon of thyme

2 cups of chopped green onions

2 pounds of shrimp, peeled and deveined

4 cups of sautéed okra

Cooked rice

Filé

Breaux Bridge Secret Gumbo

2 pounds of fresh okra, sliced

1/2 cup of oil

1 large slice of ham, diced
(about 1/4 pound)

4 medium onions, chopped

2 tablespoons of flour

1 large bellpepper, chopped

3 stalks of celery, chopped

Handful of fresh parsley, cut fine
with scissors

3 bay leaves

4 cloves of garlic, pressed

1 tablespoon of thyme

2 8-ounce cans of tomato sauce

3 quarts of boiling water

1 15 1/2-ounce can of peeled
tomatoes with juice

1 pound of lump crabmeat

6 whole boiled crabs (crack claws)

2 pounds of shrimp, peeled and
cleaned

Salt and cayenne pepper, to taste

2 pints of oysters and their liquid

Gumbo filé

Many Cajun recipes hinge on a secret. Reference books say that filé is used to bind a gumbo when okra is not available, but this is a prize-winning gumbo recipe that uses both. The cook says that his secret rests in the filé.

1. Smother okra in oil over medium-low heat in a heavy pot with a lid for 25 minutes.

2. Add diced ham and onions and cook 10 minutes.

3. Sprinkle flour over this, stir and brown the whole mixture. Add just enough water to keep it from sticking.

4. Add bellpepper, celery, parsley, bay leaves, garlic and thyme, stirring constantly.

5. Add tomato sauce and simmer five minutes. Slowly add boiling water and undrained tomatoes, stirring constantly.

6. Simmer two and a half hours.

7. During the last 20 minutes add crabs and crabmeat, shrimp, and salt and pepper. About 10 minutes before serving add oysters and liquid. Stir well and taste.

8. Add filé until gumbo barely loses its sweetness (start with one tablespoon).

Makes one and a half gallons.

David Whittaker
The Only Texas Cookbook

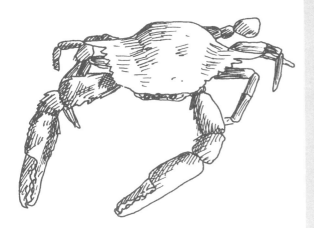

New Orleans Seafood Filé Gumbo

Seasoning Mix (Recipe follows)

1 1/2 cups of Cajun Roux
(See recipe, page 24.)

12 medium frog legs

1 large onion, chopped

1 medium bellpepper, chopped

1/2 cup of chopped celery

4 medium garlic cloves, finely
minced

4 quarts of Seafood Stock (See
recipe, page 40) or 8 8-oz. bottles
of clam juice and 2 quarts of water

2 pounds of uncooked heads-on
shrimp, peeled (Reserve heads and
shells.)

2 bay leaves

1/2 of medium lemon

1 tablespoon of minced parsley,
preferably flat-leaf

1 teaspoon of dried thyme or 1
tablespoon of chopped fresh thyme

1 teaspoon of freshly ground black
pepper

1/2 teaspoon of cayenne pepper

Salt, to taste

A unique and rich gumbo, this one is made with one of Louisiana's finest bayou delicacies: frog legs.

1. Prepare Seasoning Mix; set aside.

2. Prepare Cajun Roux as directed, cooking until mahogany-colored; set aside.

3. Using your fingers, pull meat from frog legs; lay meat on a baking sheet. Sprinkle meat with Seasoning Mix.

4. Add seasoned meat to hot roux. Cook, stirring, until lightly browned, about five minutes.

5. Add onion, bellpepper, celery and garlic; cook until onion is wilted and transparent, about five minutes.

6. Meanwhile, in a large saucepan, bring stock or clam juice and water to a boil. Tie reserved shrimp heads and shells and bay leaves in a cheesecloth bag. Add bag and lemon half to boiling stock.

7. Slowly whisk roux into boiling stock until all has been added.

8. Add parsley, thyme, black pepper, cayenne and salt.

9. Reduce heat; simmer one hour. Remove and discard cheesecloth bag and lemon half.

10. Add shrimp, crabmeat, fish and scallops. Cook over medium heat 15 minutes.

11. Taste for seasoning; adjust if necessary.

12. Spoon about half a cup of rice in each soup plate; spoon gumbo over top.

13. Add about one quarter teaspoon of filé to each bowl. Sprinkle each serving with chopped green onion and parsley.

Note: Eighteen shucked oysters or a half pound of lump crabmeat may be substituted for the frog legs. If so, add this to the gumbo along with the other seafood, and omit the Seasoning Mix.

Makes 8 to 10 servings.

SEASONING MIX

Mix all ingredients together in a small bowl.

Terry Thompson
Cajun-Creole Cooking

---

1 pound of lump crabmeat

1 pound of skinned redfish fillets, or any mild, white-fleshed fish, cut into bite-sized chunks

1/2 pound of tiny scallops

5 cups of hot cooked rice

3 1/2 tablespoons of filé

Chopped green onions

Minced parsley

1/2 teaspoon each of salt, freshly ground black pepper, cayenne pepper, paprika, onion powder and garlic powder

Acadian Seafood Filé Gumbo

3/4 cup of oil

3/4 cup of flour

2 stalks of celery, chopped

1/4 cup of chopped bellpepper

1 large onion, chopped

2 to 3 pods of garlic, minced

3 quarts of water

1 quart of seafood stock
(or 2 bottles of clam juice)

3 chicken bouillon cubes

2 pounds of shrimp,
raw and peeled

1 pound of filet of fish (redfish,
catfish or trout can be used)

1/2 cup of parsley

1/2 cup of green onion tops

1 pound of crabmeat

1 pint of oysters (shucked)
with juice

Salt, black pepper and cayenne,
to taste

6 drops of Tabasco sauce

Gumbo filé

1. In a Dutch oven or heavy skillet, heat three-fourths cup of oil over medium-high heat until it is hot. Slowly add the flour, stirring constantly to make a roux. Cook until the flour turns a dark brown (chocolate). Be careful not to burn the roux or yourself.

2. Add the celery, bellpepper, and onion to the roux. Add a little stock, then transfer the mixture to a stock pot. Add the garlic, water, seafood stock, and chicken bouillon cubes.

3. Cook over medium heat for one hour. The gumbo pot should be uncovered. Add the shrimp, fish fillets, parsley, and green onion tops. Cook for 15 minutes.

4. Add the crabmeat. Cook for 10 minutes. Then add the oysters and cook until the edges curl. Season with salt, black pepper, cayenne, and Tabasco, to taste.

5. Offer gumbo filé to each guest at the table, if desired.

6. To serve, mound rice in gumbo bowls; ladle some gumbo over the rice, and garnish with parsley. (Be sure that each guest receives shrimp, fish, oyster and crabmeat.)

Bea Weber
Abbeville, La.

Creole Seafood Gumbo

1. Melt butter in saucepan. Blend-in flour and cook over low heat, stirring constantly until dark brown.

2. Add liquid, okra, tomatoes, onion, pepper, Tabasco, thyme and bay leaf.

3. Bring to a boil. Cover and simmer 30 minutes, stirring occasionally.

4. Add seafood and cook 10 to 15 minutes longer. Remove bay leaf. Serve in soup bowls with mound of hot rice in center.

Serves six.

From The Land of Tabasco Sauce
The McIlhenny Company
Avery Island, La.

1/4 cup of butter or margarine

2 tablespoons of all-purpose flour

2 cups of liquid (water and a little juice from seafood)

2 cups of cut okra, fresh, frozen or canned

2 cups of peeled and cubed tomatoes, fresh or canned

1 large onion, chopped

1 small bellpepper, chopped

1 teaspoon of Tabasco sauce

1/8 teaspoon of thyme

1 bay leaf

2 cups of shrimp, crab meat, oysters, or a combination, fresh, frozen or canned

3 cups of hot cooked rice

Louisiana Seafood Gumbo

3 large tablespoons of oil

3 large tablespoons of flour

2 pounds of shrimp, peeled and deveined

2 quarts of water

Salt, black pepper and red pepper

2 large onions, chopped

1 can of tomatoes

3 pods of garlic, minced

1/2 pint of oysters

1 can of crabmeat

Several whole crabs and their claws, cleaned

1/2 cup of finely chopped parsley

1/2 cup of finely chopped green onion tops

1. Make roux of oil and flour, stirring constantly until dark brown.

2. Add shrimp to roux and cook for a few minutes longer.

3. Add water, salt and pepper, onion, tomatoes and garlic and simmer for about 30 minutes.

4. Add oysters, crabmeat and whole crabs and simmer until crabs are cooked, about 20 minutes.

5. Add parsley and green onions. Serve over rice. Let each person add fresh filé to his/her taste.

"Cajun Creole Cookery"
The Daily Iberian

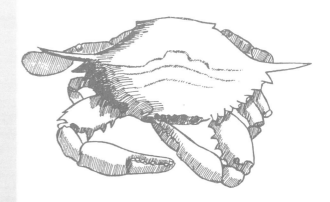

Bayou Seafood Gumbo

It's a myth that you have to live near a bayou in Louisiana or in a coastal city to enjoy a dish like Bayou Seafood Gumbo. Ranchers' and farmers' wives across the country, with homes surrounded by wheat, corn and soybean fields, also like to serve such treats for the main dish at their guest luncheons.

1. In a kettle, cook onion in butter until tender.

2. Drain and rinse shrimp in cold water.

3. Add soups, clam juice, shrimp and crab meat to onion. Heat almost to boiling.

4. Add okra with the liquid from it; bring to boiling. Reduce heat and simmer gently 10 minutes.

5. Add sherry just before serving.

6. To serve, mound a half cup of rice in center of each soup plate. Pour gumbo around rice.

Makes six to eight servings.

Nell B. Nichols, Editor
America's Best Vegetable Recipes

1/3 cup of chopped onion

2 tablespoons of butter

2 5-ounce cans of shrimp

1 can of condensed tomato soup

2 cans of condensed Manhattan clam chowder

1 1/2 cups of canned clam juice or chicken broth

1 5- to 7-ounce can of crab meat

1 (1-pound) can of cut okra

2 tablespoons of dry sherry

3 to 4 cups of hot cooked rice

Seafood Gumbo, Southern Style

1/4 cup of flour

2 tablespoons of vegetable oil

1 1/2 cups of chopped onion

1 cup of chopped celery

1/2 medium bellpepper, chopped

1 clove of garlic, minced

5 cups of chicken broth

1 28-ounce can of tomatoes, crushed

1 6-ounce can of tomato paste

2 teaspoons of salt

1 teaspoon of bouquet garni*

1/4 teaspoon of ground red pepper

1/4 teaspoon of ground black pepper

1 pound of fish fillets, cut in 1 1/2-inch pieces

1 pound of peeled, deveined raw shrimp

1 10-ounce package of frozen sliced okra

1 1/2 teaspoons of gumbo filé

6 cups of hot cooked rice

1. Blend flour and oil in Dutch oven or large pot, preferably cast iron. Cook, stirring constantly, until roux turns a deep brown.

2. Add onion, celery, bellpepper and garlic and continue cooking until onion is transparent.

3. Add broth, tomatoes, tomato paste, and seasonings. Cover and simmer about 30 minutes.

4. Add fish, shrimp and okra. Cover and cook 10 minutes longer, or until shrimp turn pink.

5. Adjust seasonings, if necessary. Stir-in filé. (Do not boil once filé is added.)

6. Serve in shallow bowls with hot cooked rice.

Makes 12 servings.

* Bouquet garni is a combination of herbs such as marjoram, sage, basil, thyme, rosemary and oregano placed in a cheesecloth bag or a tea ball. A prepared blend may also be purchased.

USA Rice Council

Seafood Filé Gumbo
(A Microwave Recipe)

1. In a four-quart casserole dish make a roux with flour and oil. (Cook for 15 minutes for this size dish.)

2. Sauté onion and celery on high for three minutes, then add green onions, parsley and garlic, and sauté for three minutes.

3. Stir-in water and seasonings. Cover and cook on high for 15 minutes.

4. Add shrimp and crabs, reduce to medium and cook for 25 minutes.

5. Add oysters and juice, and cook for 10 minutes or until oysters curl.

6. Sprinkle with filé. Set aside until ready to serve. Reheat gently.

Jeanne H. Landry
Sauté: A Collection Of Creole Recipes For The Microwave Oven

1/2 cup of flour

1/2 cup of oil

2 cups of chopped onion

1/2 cup of chopped celery

1/2 cup of chopped green onions

1/2 cup of chopped parsley

6 toes of garlic, chopped

1 1/2 quarts of water

1 tablespoon of salt

1 teaspoon of black pepper

1/2 teaspoon of cayenne pepper

2 pounds of shrimp, peeled

1 pound of crabmeat or 6 small seasoned boiled crabs, cleaned

1 dozen oysters, with juice

1 tablespoon filé

Seafood Gumbo
For Large Gatherings

10 smoked sausages, cut into 2-inch pieces

1 cup of cooking oil

100 gallons of hot water

10 pounds of ham, chopped

105 pounds of raw shrimp, peeled

52 onions, chopped

10 pods of garlic, minced

17 bellpeppers, chopped

1 bottle of soy sauce

10 stalks of celery, chopped

1 cup of flour

3 bottles of Red Devil sauce

115 pounds of crab meat

4 gallons of raw oysters

Filé

Cooked rice

1. Fry smoked sausage in a large skillet. Remove from pan and drain.

2. Put cooking oil into a very large gumbo pot or pots.*

3. Gradually add 100 gallons of hot water.

4. Fry ham and add to water and oil along with shrimp, onion, garlic, bellpepper, soy sauce, celery, flour and Red Devil sauce. Cook for two hours, stirring occasionally.

5. Add crab meat and cook 15 minutes more.

6. Add raw oysters and cook just until the edges curl.

7. When ready to serve, sprinkle filé over the individual servings. Serve with rice.

Serves 150.

*Note: If two or three pots are used, simply divide the ingredients proportionally between them.

Mary Land's Louisiana Cookery

The Mariner's Gumbo

A seafood gumbo culinary masterpiece!

1. Cook bacon in large, heavy pot and remove.

2. Add vegetables and sauté until tender. Add spices, water, tomatoes and okra and cook 30 minutes.

3. Add seafood, bacon (crumbled) and wine and cook another 30 minutes.

4. Serve over hot rice.

Makes 10 to 14 servings.

Note: Gumbo is a hearty main course with a salad and french bread, but it is also most elegant served in a cup before dinner with little or no rice. Your guests will be so pleased with this elegant first course that the entree will have a tough act to follow!

Gwen McKee
The Little Gumbo Book

---

5 strips of raw bacon

1 cup of chopped onion

1/2 cup of chopped bellpepper

1/2 cup of chopped celery

1 teaspoon of minced garlic

1 teaspoon each: thyme, oregano, basil, black pepper, chili powder and Tabasco

2 1/2 quarts of water

1 28-ounce can of tomatoes, chopped

1 pound of cut okra

1 pound of diced fresh fish fillets (catfish, flounder, redfish)

2 pounds of raw, peeled shrimp

1/2 pound of cooked, diced scallops

1/2 pound of fresh picked crab meat (optional)

1/2 cup of white wine

Southern Gumbo

1 cup of vegetable oil

1 cup of all-purpose flour

8 stalks of celery

3 large onions, chopped

1 bellpepper, chopped

2 cloves of garlic, minced

1/2 cup of chopped fresh parsley (optional)

2 tablespoons of vegetable oil

1 pound of okra, sliced

2 quarts of chicken stock

2 quarts of water

1/2 cup of Worcestershire sauce

Hot sauce, to taste

1/2 cup of catsup

1 large tomato, chopped

1 tablespoon of salt

4 slices of bacon or 1 large ham slice, chopped

1 or 2 bay leaves

1/4 teaspoon of dried thyme

1/4 teaspoon of dried rosemary

1. Combine oil and flour in a large Dutch oven; cook over medium heat, stirring constantly, until roux is the color of a copper penny (10 to 15 minutes).

2. Stir-in celery, onion, bell-pepper and garlic; also add parsley, if desired. Cook an additional 45 minutes to one hour, stirring occasionally. (You can cut cooking time at this stage, but the gumbo won't taste as good.)

3. Fry okra in two tablespoons of hot oil until brown. Add to gumbo; stir well over low heat for a few minutes. (At this stage, the mixture may be cooled, packaged and frozen or refrigerated for later use, if you wish.)

4. Add the next 12 ingredients; simmer two and a half to three hours, stirring occasionally.

5. About 30 minutes before serving, add chicken, crabmeat and shrimp; simmer 30 minutes.

6. Add oysters, if desired, during last 10 minutes of simmering period. Stir-in molasses.

7. Serve over rice.

Makes about seven and a half quarts.

Susan Payne
"Cooking In The Cajun Style "
Creative Ideas For Living

Red pepper flakes, to taste (optional)

2 cups of chopped cooked chicken

1 or 2 pounds of fresh crabmeat

4 pounds of shrimp, peeled and deveined

1 pint of oysters, undrained (optional)

1 teaspoon of molasses or brown sugar

Hot cooked rice

24-Karat Gumbo

2 pounds of raw shrimp in shells

3 quarts of water

3 lemon slices

3 bay leaves

1 teaspoon of K's Cajun Seasoning
or salt and pepper

2/3 cup of flour

1/2 cup of vegetable oil

2 cups of chopped onion

1 cup of chopped celery

1/2 cup of chopped bellpepper

1 16-ounce can of tomatoes,
chopped

3 10-ounce packages of frozen cut
okra

2 teaspoons of minced garlic

2 tablespoons each: chopped
parsley, Tabasco, Worcestershire

1 1/2 teaspoons each: salt, black
pepper, dried basil

2 cups of cooked chicken, torn to
bite-size pieces

4 crabs with claws, cleaned and
quartered (or 12 ounces of picked
crab meat)

12 to 16 oysters with liquid

Filé

Chopped green onions

Rich . . . in every sense of the word

1. Boil shrimp in water with lemon, bay leaves and "K's." Boil one minute, then remove shrimp to platter to cool.

2. Discard lemon and bay leaves; reserve stock. Make roux by browning flour and oil. Add roux to stock pot along with remaining ingredients except seafood, filé and green onions; simmer 30 minutes.

3. Peel shrimp and add to stock with other seafood. Cook gently 20 to 30 minutes.

4. Serve over rice.

5. Put filé and green onions on table for whomever wants them.

Serves 12 to 15.

Note: This 24-ingredient gumbo is truly a feast! A little more trouble, a little more expense, but well worth it!

Gwen McKee
The Little Gumbo Book

Moulin-Rouge Gumbo

If you can open a can, you can make this gumbo!

1. In a Dutch oven, brown butter and flour lightly on medium heat.

2. Stir-in remaining ingredients except seafood and filé.

3. Bring to a boil, lower heat and simmer 20 to 30 minutes.

4. Add seafood with all juices and filé; stir and simmer another 10 minutes.

5. Remove from heat, cover and let sit another 30 minutes. Serve over rice in bowls.

Serves four to six.

Gwen McKee
The Little Gumbo Book

1/2 stick of butter or margarine

2 tablespoons of flour

1 1-pound can of okra

1 11-ounce can of chicken broth

1 12-ounce can of tomato juice

2 juice cans of water

1 5-ounce can of boned chicken

1/2 teaspoon of K's Cajun Seasoning, or salt, black pepper and red pepper

3 tablespoons of dried chipped onions

1/2 teaspoon of garlic (granulated, powdered or fresh minced)

3 6-ounce cans of seafood (shrimp, clams, crab meat; any combination)

1 teaspoon of filé

Black's Oyster Bar Gumbo

2 pints of Mazola Corn Oil

3 pints of flour

1 tablespoon of tomato paste

3 1/4 pounds of onions, diced

3 1/4 pounds of celery, diced

3 1/2 gallons of oyster liquid, divided

1 teaspoon of Worcestershire sauce

3 tablespoons of Louisiana Hot Sauce

1 tablespoon of Tabasco sauce

1 tablespoon of white pepper

1 tablespoon of black pepper

1 tablespoon of red pepper

1/2 cup of salt

3 quarts of peeled shrimp, divided (Reserve heads and shells.)

2 1/2 gallons of shrimp stock

1 pint of chopped bellpepper

Rind of 3 lemons

This recipe from Abbeville's famous Black's Oyster Bar will feed a crowd or stock your freezer for the winter.

1. In a large Magnalite roasting pan, heat oil on the highest heat possible until the oil smokes. Do not burn the oil. Add the flour. (Enough flour should be added so that when a spoon is drawn through the mixture, the flour appears to follow behind the spoon in its wake.) Constantly stir the roux until it is dark brown. Add the tomato paste.

2. To the roux add the onion and celery. Add two gallons of oyster liquid. (Use the remaining oyster liquid throughout preparation to maintain the liquid volume.) Simmer for five minutes.

3. Add the Worcestershire sauce, Louisiana Hot Sauce, Tabasco, white pepper, black pepper, red pepper and salt. Simmer one and one half hours, stirring occasionally.

4. Add the reserved shrimp heads and shells to two and one-half gallons of water. Simmer for one half hour.

5. Strain the shrimp stock and add it to the gumbo. Add additional oyster liquid as needed. Cook for one and one half hours on medium heat.

6. Add the chopped bellpepper. Cook for another 30 minutes.

7. Add the lemon rinds. Cook for 30 minutes.

8. Divide the six gallons of gumbo into three two-gallon containers and cool. Refrigerate or freeze until ready to serve.

9. To serve, add to one of the two-gallon containers one quart of oysters, one quart of shrimp and one and one-half pounds of claw crabmeat. Simmer for 15 minutes.

10. Serve immediately over hot cooked rice, or refrigerate until needed and reheat in a micro-wave oven until steaming. (A cup serving should contain two oysters and three shrimp. A bowl should have five oysters and five shrimp.)

11. Garnish each serving with onion tops. (Delicious with potato salad!)

Makes six gallons.

Bryan Bourque
Black's Oyster Bar
Abbeville, La.

3 quarts of oysters, divided

4 1/2 pounds of claw crabmeat, divided

Green onion tops, chopped

Seafood Gumbo With Chicken

1 4- to 5-pound hen or 2 frying chickens, cut into serving pieces

1 28-ounce can of tomatoes

6 tablespoons of bacon drippings

6 tablespoons of flour

4 medium onions, finely chopped

2 or 3 bellpeppers, finely chopped

1/2 medium stalk of celery, finely chopped

1 1/2 quarts of boiling water

Salt, black pepper, Worcestershire and cayenne, to taste

1 pound of shrimp, shelled and deveined

1 1/2 pounds of okra, cut

Filé

Cooked rice (optional)

Some people like whole dressed crabs in gumbo. If so, about six to eight, added along with crabmeat, will give a stronger crab flavor. When oysters are in season, a pint of oysters may also be added. This gumbo can be frozen and kept for six weeks to two months. Filé should not be added until gumbo is reheated and ready for serving.

1. Simmer chicken in water to cover until tender. Remove to cool.

2. Mash meaty parts of tomatoes; add tomatoes and their liquid to chicken stock.

3. Heat bacon drippings in a skillet. Stir-in flour; cook until lightly browned. Add onion, bellpepper and celery. Continue to cook until dark brown. Add boiling water. Simmer for 10 minutes.

4. Stir vegetable mixture gradually into chicken stock. Season with salt and pepper, a little Worcestershire and dash of cayenne.

5. Add seafood and okra; cover; simmer for two hours, stirring occasionally.

6. Add enough filé to thicken and add flavor. Simmer for 10 minutes longer.

7. If desired, serve with rice.

Serves 12 to 15.

Louise C. Stamps
The General Federation of Women's
Clubs Cookbook, *America Cooks*

Seafood, Sausage & Chicken Filé Gumbo

1 3-pound chicken, cut up

1 pound of andouille sausage or Creole smoked sausage, chopped fine

2 pounds of heads-on shrimp (or 2 pounds of frozen tails)

1/2 cup of butter

1/2 cup of flour

2 large onions, chopped

1/2 cup of celery leaves, chopped fine

4 green onions with their green leaves, chopped fine

1/2 teaspoon of thyme

1 bay leaf

1/4 teaspoon of cayenne

Salt and freshly ground black pepper, to taste

3 dozen oysters and their liquid

Filé powder

Steamed rice

1. Place the cut-up chicken pieces in a pot, add the chopped sausage, cover with water, and add a teaspoon of salt. Boil for 45 minutes.

2. Remove the chicken and sausage and reserve the broth. Remove the chicken meat from the bones, dice it, and set it aside.

3. Wash the shrimp, cover with water in a pot, add a little salt, and boil for five minutes. Remove the shrimp from the pot, peel, and set aside. Return the heads and shells to the shrimp broth in the pot and boil vigorously for 15 minutes. Strain this broth into the chicken broth.

4. Make a roux with the butter and flour. When the roux is browned, add the onion, celery leaves and green onions. Cook slowly until the vegetables are soft and transparent.

5. Stir-in the thyme, bay leaf, cayenne and black pepper.

6. Place the roux-vegetable mix, sausage and chicken in a stew pot and cover by one inch with the chicken-shrimp broth, adding water or chicken bouillon if necessary. Simmer for one hour.

7. Add the shrimp, oysters and oyster liquid, and cook for 10 minutes longer. Adjust the salt.

8. Turn off the heat and let the gumbo sit for five minutes. (You can either add two tablespoons of filé powder and stir it in well or place the filé bottle on the table and let the guests add their own. About a half teaspoon per bowl is average.)

9. Serve in preheated gumbo bowls with a little rice in the bottom of each bowl. French bread on the side and a dry red wine are called for.

Serves eight.

Howard Mitcham
Creole Gumbo And All That Jazz

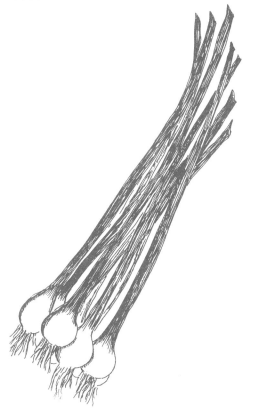

Seafood-Okra Gumbo

2 pounds of raw medium shrimp

2 quarts of water

2 thin slices of lemon

2 small bay leaves

1/2 teaspoon of peppercorns

1 teaspoon of salt

3 dozen medium oysters and their liquid (about 1 pint)

3 rounded tablespoons of lard

2 1/2 pounds of young okra cut in 1/8-inch slices

1 large onion, chopped

1 bellpepper, seeded and chopped

3 cloves of garlic, minced

1 rounded tablespoon of flour

3 cups of canned tomatoes, partially drained

1 generous bouquet garni of fresh parsley and thyme

2 pounds of well-picked crabmeat

Salt and pepper, to taste

This dish is typical of the Creole gumbos.

1. Cook shrimp until pink in two quarts of water with slices of lemon, one bay leaf, peppercorns and salt.

2. Shell and devein shrimp, reserving the broth in which they were cooked. Strain broth and combine it with the oyster liquid, setting the oysters aside. Add water if necessary to make up two and a half quarts of liquid.

3. Heat lard in a heavy pot and add the okra, onion, bellpepper and garlic. Cook over lowest heat 25 minutes, stirring frequently. (The vegetables will be done when the okra stops "roping"–throwing the characteristic thick gummy substance.) Watch that it does not burn.

4. Add flour and brown.

5. Add tomatoes and blend. Stir-in reserved broth. Add bouquet garni and the second bay leaf, shrimp, and crabmeat.

6. Cook 45 minutes over lowest heat.

7. Correct seasoning with salt and pepper as needed. Add oysters and cook until plump.

8. Serve from tureen, with fluffy rice on the side.

Serves 8 to 10.

Morton G. Clark
*French-American Cooking
From New Orleans To Quebec*

Seafood-Okra Gumbo
(A Microwave Recipe)

1. In a four-quart casserole dish stir-in a fourth cup of oil, tomatoes, onion, garlic and okra. Cook covered on high for one hour. Stir occasionally.

2. In a two-cup measuring cup, make roux, with a fourth cup of oil and a fourth cup of flour, add to okra mixture along with water and seasonings. Bring to a boil for 15 minutes.

3. Stir-in shrimp and crabs. Cook on medium for 30 minutes.

4. Serve hot over rice. Always offer a shaker of filé and green hot pepper.

*Microwave ovens will not 'smother' vegetables in the conventional way. However, anyone who has stirred a large pot of okra for gumbo will appreciate this method. Be prepared for a different look, but the flavor is the same.

Jeanne H. Landry
Sauté: A Collection of Creole Recipes For The Microwave Oven

1/2 cup of oil, divided

1 can of tomatoes

2 cups of chopped onion

6 toes of garlic, chopped

1 package of frozen sliced okra or 2 pounds of fresh okra, sliced*

1/4 cup of flour

1 1/2 quarts of water

1 tablespoon of salt

1/2 teaspoon of pepper

1/2 teaspoon of cayenne

2 pounds of shrimp, peeled

1 pound of crabmeat or 6 small boiled crabs, cleaned

Creole Gumbo

4 tablespoons of butter

4 tablespoons of flour

3 large onions, chopped

2 bellpeppers, chopped

6 green onions with their leaves, chopped

4 cloves of garlic, minced

1 cup of chopped celery

3 pounds of fresh okra, sliced (or 4 packages of frozen)

4 strips of bacon

1/2 pound of country ham, diced

1 pound of stewing beef, diced small

1 chicken, about 2 pounds, cut into serving pieces

5 pounds of fresh heads-on shrimp or 4 pounds of frozen shrimp tails

The operation requires several utensils, a big skillet, a big stew pot, and several smaller pots for steaming.

1. For the roux, melt the butter in the skillet, add the flour, and stir until dark brown, keeping the fire very low.

2. To the roux, add the chopped onion, bellpepper, green onion, garlic and celery and stir them in well. Adding more butter if necessary, cook the vegetables until they're limp and transparent, but don't brown them.

3. Add the okra and keep cooking until the okra loses its gummy consistency. Put this mixture into the large stew pot.

4. Clean the skillet, and fry the strips of bacon and the ham slowly until browned. Add the ham to the pot, and drain the bacon on a paper towel. Crumble it and add to the pot.

5. Shake the stewing beef in a paper bag with seasoned flour, coating it well, and add it to the bacon grease in the skillet. Sear the beef until it's browned on all sides, and add it to the pot.

6. Place the chicken in a pot, and cover with water, adding a teaspoon of salt. Boil for 30 to 40 minutes, or until tender.

7. Remove the chicken and add its cooking stock to the big pot. Remove the skin from the chicken, cut the skin into very small pieces, and add it to the pot. Remove the chicken meat from the bones, dice it, and add it to the pot.

8. Wash the shrimp and cover them with water in a pot, adding a little salt. Bring to a boil and cook for five minutes, or until they're pink and easy to peel.

9. Take the shrimp out and cool them in the sink. Set aside the shrimp stock in the pot. Peel the shrimp and set them aside.

10. Take the heads and the shells off the shrimp, place them in a flat-bottomed container, and crush them thoroughly with a pestle or an empty bottle. Pour this mixture into the shrimp water in the pot, and boil it vigorously for 15 minutes.

11. Strain the liquid through triple cheesecloth into the big stew pot. (The stuff inside the shrimp's head is like the tomalley of a lobster—a nectar of the gods—and this stock will really give kick to the gumbo.)

12. Wash the live crabs thoroughly, put them in a pot, cover with boiling water, and boil for 20 minutes.

13. Remove the crabs and pour

12 live crabs or 1 pound of frozen crabmeat

4 dozen oysters and their liquid

4 large Creole tomatoes, peeled and diced (or a 32-ounce can)

1/4 cup of chopped parsley

1 meaty ham bone

2 bay leaves

1 teaspoon of thyme

2 tablespoons of Worcestershire

1/2 teaspoon of cayenne

1 teaspoon of freshly ground black pepper

6 quarts of stock or water (or more)

4 tablespoons of salt (or more)

Cooked rice

the stock into the large stew pot.

14. Clean the crabs. Remove the top shells and scrape the spongy gills off. Break off the mouth parts, and remove the "apron" on the bottom of the crab. Twist off the fins, legs and claws.

15. Crack the claws and put them in the main pot. Break the body into two halves and drop them in. (Be sure you've scraped out all the crab fat from the corners of the top shells and from the body cavity and added it to the pot, because a gumbo wouldn't be fit to eat without this delicious stuff!)

16. Crush the crab shells, legs, and fins in the bottom of a pot as you did the shrimp shells. Cover them with water and boil vigorously for 15 minutes. Strain the liquid and add it to the main cooking pot.

17. Add the oyster liquid to the pot. Get as much of this from your oyster dealer as you can, a quart or two if possible, but if you can't get that much, the chicken, shrimp, and crab stock (plus water if needed) will do.

18. Heat the ingredients in the main cooking pot.

19. Add the tomatoes, parsley and ham bone, plus all the flavoring elements except the salt. The liquid should cover everything in the pot by about two inches, so add more liquid if necessary. (You can use fish stock, oyster liquid, chicken bouillon, a combination of all these, or just plain water.)

20. Bring what's in the pot to a boil, then lower the heat, place an asbestos pad under the pot to prevent scorching, and boil gently for one and a half to two hours. (The longer it cooks, the better.)

21. Stir it occasionally and scrape the bottom with a metal kitchen spoon. (If there's a black residue on the tip of your spoon, it means you're scorching it, and you'd better slow down. If it really begins to burn and has an acrid, scorched smell, you must cut off the heat, remove the gumbo from the pot, clean all the burned material off the bottom of the pot, rinse it out, put the gumbo back in, and start cooking again. A stew containing roux will always scorch if you don't keep a close watch on it and cook slowly.)

22. About 30 minutes before the gumbo is done, start cooking your rice. Bring 12 cups of water to a boil, and add a tablespoon of vegetable oil, four teaspoons of salt and five cups of rice. Stir the mixture vigorously, and when it returns to a boil, turn the heat very low. Cover the pot tightly and cook for 15 to 20 minutes or until all the water is absorbed. Let the rice set for a few minutes, and then taste for doneness.

(Never stir steaming rice until it's done.)

23. Ten minutes before serving the gumbo, add the shrimp and the oysters to the pot, and stir them in.

24. Keep adding salt to the pot and stirring it in until it achieves a deep, rich savor. (A good gumbo must have plenty of salt in it if it's to be as savory as it should be.)

25. Serve the gumbo in large preheated soup bowls. Place a half cup of rice in the bottom of each bowl and ladle the gumbo over it, making sure that each bowl gets a generous share of all the elements—shrimp, crab and oysters. (Option: Many hosts prefer to pass around a bowl of hot rice and let the guests add the amount they want.)

Serves 12 or more.

Note: I like a good full-bodied imported red Burgundy with my gumbo, but many prefer the lighter white wines.

Howard Mitcham,
Creole Gumbo And All That Jazz

Shrimp Gumbo

3 tablespoons of bacon drippings

1 medium onion, chopped

3 tablespoons of flour

1 can of tomato sauce

1/2 pound of okra, chopped

1/2 cup of chopped celery

A few sprigs of parsley, chopped

1 quart of water

1/2 teaspoon of poultry seasoning

1/4 teaspoon of black pepper

1 teaspoon of salt

2 teaspoons of Worcestershire sauce

1 pound of shrimp, peeled

1. Heat bacon drippings in skillet and sauté onion until limp.

2. Add flour and brown for roux. Add tomato sauce, okra, celery and parsley, stirring constantly until mixture is very thick.

3. Have a quart of water boiling in large sauce pan. Pour contents from skillet into boiling water.

4. Add seasonings and shrimp. Cook slowly for about one hour.

5. Serve with cooked rice.

Note: More water may be added if it boils down too low. Crab meat may be added if desired.

Serves four.

Mrs. William Pettey
The Gulf Gourmet: Recipes From The Mississippi Coast

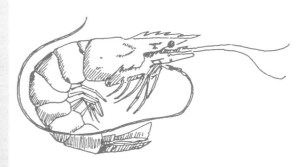

Shrimp Filé Gumbo

1. Scald the shrimp in boiling water and season highly.

2. Heat the shortening in a large kettle and, when hot, add the flour, making a brown roux.

3. When quite brown, without a semblance of burning, add the onion and the parsley. Fry these, and when brown, add the bay leaf and thyme; pour in the oyster liquid and the hot water, or use the carefully strained liquid in which the shrimp were boiled.

4. When it comes to a good boil, and about five minutes before serving, add the shrimp to the gumbo and take it off the stove.

5. Add to the boiling hot liquid about two heaping tablespoonfuls of the filé, thickening according to taste.

6. Season again with salt and pepper. Serve immediately with cooked rice.

The Times-Picayune
The Picayune Original Creole Cookbook

---

50 shrimp, deheaded, shelled and washed

1 tablespoonful of shortening or 2 tablespoons of butter

1 tablespoon of flour

1 large white onion, chopped

3 sprigs of parsley, chopped

1 bay leaf, chopped

1 sprig of thyme

2 quarts of oyster liquid

1 quart of hot water

2 tablespoons of filé

Salt and black pepper, to taste

Dash of cayenne

Louisiana Shrimp Gumbo

1/2 cup of butter, margarine, or oil

2/3 cup of flour

2 cups of chopped onion

1 cup of chopped celery

1 cup of chopped bellpepper

4 cloves of garlic, minced

1/2 cup of sliced green onion tops, divided

1/4 cup of snipped fresh parsley

2 bay leaves

1 teaspoon of salt

1/2 teaspoon of ground black pepper

Ground red pepper, to taste

2 quarts of hot chicken broth or water

2 pounds of raw shrimp, peeled and deveined

3 to 4 cups of hot cooked rice

Filé

1. Melt butter in large heavy pot (cast iron preferred). Blend-in flour and stir over medium-low heat until roux is dark brown.

2. Add onion, celery and bellpepper; cook until vegetables are soft.

3. Stir-in garlic, a fourth cup of onion tops, parsley and seasonings; add hot broth. Simmer for two hours.

4. Add shrimp and cook 10 minutes.

5. Stir-in remaining fourth cup of onion tops. Remove bay leaves.

6. Ladle gumbo into bowls. Stir-in small amount of filé (one-eighth teaspoon per cup) and top each with a mound of rice.

Makes 10 servings. (Approximately 10 cups of gumbo)

USA Rice Council

Shrimp & Crab Gumbo

1. Sauté shrimp and crabmeat with two tablespoons of the shortening in a large pot; add water and set aside.

2. In remaining two tablespoons of the shortening, sauté onion, garlic, bellpepper and celery slightly; add okra and continue sautéing until brown.

3. Add vegetables to seafood, along with the tomato sauce and seasonings; stir well to remove all browned particles from the bottom of the pot.

4. Cook slowly for about two hours.

5. Add parsley. Serve over cooked rice.

Serves six to eight.

Mrs. Mary Pryolo
Lafourche Parish, La.

2 pounds of shrimp, peeled and deveined

1/2 dozen crabs, boiled and peeled

1/4 cup of shortening

2 quarts of water

1 large onion, chopped

1 garlic clove, minced

1 bellpepper, chopped

1 stalk of celery, chopped

2 pounds of okra, fresh or frozen (if fresh, slice and fry)

1 can of tomato sauce

1 bay leaf

1 tablespoon of Worcestershire sauce

Salt and pepper, to taste

Parsley, chopped

Cooked rice

Shrimp & Crab Filé Gumbo

1/2 cup of peanut oil

2 tablespoons of bacon drippings

2 cups of chopped onions

1/4 cup of chopped bellpepper

1/2 cup of chopped celery

2 teaspoons of chopped garlic

8 ounces of tomato sauce

2 bay leaves

1 teaspoon of sugar

1/2 teaspoon of crab boil, store-bought or homemade (Recipe follows)

5 tablespoons of browned flour (dark dry roux)

10 cups of hot water

Salt and pepper

12 crabs, raw and cleaned

2 pounds of shrimp, cleaned

3 tablespoons of filé powder

A popular Louisiana gumbo is one made with filé (fee-lay). This herb, inherited from the Louisiana Choctaw Indians, is the product of grinding and sifting of dried sassafras leaves into a fine powder. It not only imparts a unique flavor to the gumbo but acts as a thickening agent just as the okra does in the Okra Gumbo. Its flavor is very spicy, somewhat hot but not peppery. Filé should never be added to the gumbo while it is cooking since at boiling temperatures it will make the gumbo stringy and unpalatable.

1. Sauté onions, bellpepper, celery and garlic in oil and bacon fat until onions are well done.

2. Add tomato sauce. Cook slowly about 10 minutes.

3. Add bay leaves, sugar, crab boil, flour, water, salt and pepper. Simmer about 10 minutes.

4. Sauté crabs in small amount of oil until brown. Sauté shrimp in oil until brown. Add crabs and shrimp to gumbo.

5. Simmer about 10 minutes. Remove from heat.

6. Add filé powder. Let rest for a half-hour. Reheat (do not boil).

7. Serve over cooked rice.

CRAB BOIL

1. Blend all ingredients.

2. Bring to a boil. Reduce until liquid is one-third cup.

3. Strain.

Chef Earl Peyroux
Gourmet Cooking by Earl Peyroux

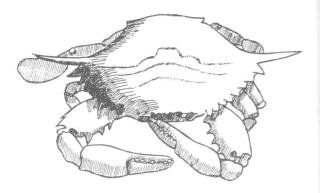

2 teaspoons of mustard seed	
1 teaspoon of coriander seed	
1/4 teaspoon of cayenne pepper	
3 bay leaves	
1/2 teaspoon of dill seed	
1/2 teaspoon of allspice	
1/2 teaspoon of cloves	
3/4 cup of water	

Shrimp & Okra Gumbo

Salt, black pepper and cayenne pepper, to taste

2 pounds of shrimp, peeled, deveined and cut in halves

2 1/2 pounds of okra, cut in 1/2-inch pieces

6 tablespoons of Puritan oil

1 tomato, peeled and chopped fine

2 medium onions, chopped fine

2 celery ribs, sliced thin

1/4 cup of bellpepper, chopped fine

1 can of Rotel tomatoes

3 cloves of garlic, minced

1 tablespoon of tomato paste

6 green onions, minced

1 bay leaf

2 chicken bouillon cubes

1 teaspoon of white vinegar

3 quarts of water

1 bottle of clam juice

1 teaspoon of paprika

3 dashes of Tabasco sauce

1. In a bowl combine salt, black pepper and cayenne pepper. Dredge the shrimp in this seasoning. Set the shrimp aside.

2. Sauté the okra in the oil for half an hour. Add the chopped tomato, onion, celery, bellpepper, Rotel tomatoes, garlic, tomato paste, green onions, bay leaf, bouillon cubes and white vinegar. Simmer for 30 more minutes.

3. Add the water and clam juice. Season with salt, black pepper and cayenne pepper. Add one teaspoon of paprika, Tabasco, Worcestershire and mustard. Cook for 30 minutes.

4. Add shrimp. Cook 30 minutes on medium heat. Remove bay leaf and discard.

5. Add green onion tops and parsley. Cook five minutes. Adjust seasonings.

6. Darken gumbo with Kitchen Bouquet, if desired.

7. To serve, mound rice in gumbo bowls, ladle some gumbo over the rice, and garnish with parsley.

8. Offer filé at the table.

Bea Weber
Abbeville, La.

1 tablespoon of Worcestershire

1 tablespoon of French's mustard

1/4 cup of chopped green onion tops

1/4 cup of fresh, chopped parsley

1 tablespoon of Kitchen Bouquet

Hot cooked rice

Filé

Shrimp, Crab & Okra Gumbo

2 cups of raw shrimp, peeled and deveined

2 teaspoons of Tony's Creole Seasoning, divided

1 cup of vegetable oil

1 cup of all-purpose flour

2 medium onions, chopped

1/2 cup of chopped celery

1/2 cup of chopped bellpepper

1/2 cup of chopped green onion tops

6 cloves of garlic, chopped

4 cups of cut okra

4 quarts of boiling water

12 boiled and cleaned crabs

1 teaspoon of butter or margarine

1. Combine shrimp and one teaspoon of Creole seasoning; set aside.

2. In a 10-quart soup pot, make a roux with oil and flour over medium-high heat, stirring until golden brown.

3. Add shrimp, onion, celery, bellpepper, green onion, and garlic; cook for 20 minutes.

4. Add okra and one teaspoon of Creole seasoning; cook 20 minutes, stirring occasionally.

5. Add boiling water and crabs; cook on medium heat for 45 minutes, stirring often.

6. Turn heat off; add butter and cover pot until ready for use.

7. Serve with rice and hot garlic bread.

Serves 16.

Mrs. Bertha Graugnard
St. James Parish, La.

Shrimp & Egg Gumbo

1. In a heavy skillet, heat oil and gradually add flour, stirring constantly to make a dark brown roux.

2. Put water, roux, onion, bellpepper and seasonings in a large gumbo pot and boil for 30 minutes.

3. Add shrimp and eggs and cook for 45 minutes.

4. Serve with rice and hot pepper vinegar.

Serves six to eight people.

Lena Guidry
Sweetlake (Calcasieu Parish), La.

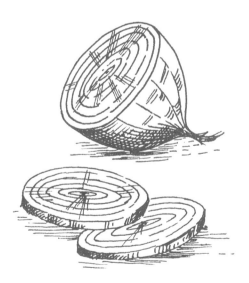

1/2 cup of oil

1/2 cup of flour

1 gallon of water

1 onion, chopped

1 bellpepper, chopped

Salt, to taste

Red pepper, to taste

1 pound of shrimp, peeled

6 hard-boiled eggs, whole

Egg & Dried Shrimp Gumbo

1 cup of finely chopped onion

1 cup of finely chopped green bellpepper

1/2 cup of finely chopped celery

2/3 cup of vegetable oil

2/3 cup of all-purpose flour

3 bay leaves

1 teaspoon of salt

3/4 teaspoon of white pepper

1/2 teaspoon of black pepper

1 1/2 teaspoons of Tabasco

3/4 cup of dried shrimp (that's two 1 1/2-ounce packages)

7 cups of seafood stock (preferred) or water

1 teaspoon of minced garlic

9 whole hard-boiled eggs, peeled

1 1/2 cups of hot cooked rice

Since fresh shrimp were not generally available where we lived we often used dried shrimp in gumbo.

1. Combine the onion, bellpepper and celery in a medium-size bowl and set aside.

2. In a large skillet (preferably not a non-stick type) heat the oil over high heat until it begins to smoke, about four minutes. Gradually add the flour, whisking constantly with a long-handled metal whisk until smooth. Continue cooking, whisking constantly, until the roux is dark red-brown to black, about three to four minutes (being careful not to let it scorch or splash on your skin). Immediately stir-in the vegetable mixture and cook about two minutes, stirring constantly.

3. Add the seasonings, bay leaves and Tabasco; cook for about two minutes, stirring almost constantly. Stir-in the shrimp, then cook about two minutes more, stirring occasionally. Remove from heat.

4. Place the stock or water and garlic in a four-quart saucepan. Bring to a boil. Stir-in the shrimp mixture until roux is dissolved. Return to a boil; reduce heat and simmer until shrimp are cooked and flavors married, about 20 minutes, stirring occasionally.

5. Add six of the whole eggs to the gumbo; cut the remaining three eggs in half and add. Turn heat to high and return mixture to a boil; then remove from heat and let sit 10 minutes.

6. Skim oil from top and serve immediately.

7. To serve, place one-fourth cup of rice in each serving bowl; add one whole egg and one egg half to each. Spoon about one cup of gumbo over the top. (It's best if each person breaks up the eggs while eating the gumbo.)

Makes six servings.

Chef Paul Prudhomme
Authentic Cajun Cooking

Shrimp & Oyster Gumbo

Salt, cayenne pepper
and black pepper, to taste

2 pounds of peeled, deveined
shrimp

1/2 cup of fat or cooking oil

3/4 cup of all-purpose flour

2 large onions, chopped

1 can of tomatoes, sieved

1 can of tomato paste

1/4 cup of bellpepper, chopped

1 cup of chopped celery

2 cloves of garlic, minced

4 quarts of water

1 bottle of clam juice

1 bouillon cube

1 1/2 teaspoons of thyme

1 pound of okra, sliced

1 bay leaf

3/4 cup of chopped,
cooked ham (6 ounces)

1. In a bowl, combine salt, black pepper and cayenne. Dredge the shrimp in this seasoning mix. Shake off any excess and set the shrimp aside.

2. In a Dutch oven or heavy skillet, heat the fat or cooking oil over medium heat until it is hot. Add the flour gradually in small amounts to make a roux. Stir continuously to avoid burning the roux.

3. Add the onions, tomatoes, tomato paste, bellpepper, celery and garlic. Sauté, stirring occasionally, until the onions appear transparent, about five minutes.

4. Add water, clam juice, bouillon cube, thyme, okra, bay leaf; increase the heat to high and bring to a boil, stirring frequently. Reduce the heat to medium-low and simmer for one hour.

5. Add the shrimp and ham and cook over medium to low heat in uncovered pot for 20 minutes.

6. Add oysters and their liquid and cook until the oyster edges curl.

7. Add parsley and green onion tops.

8. Adjust seasonings to taste, using salt, cayenne pepper, black pepper and Tabasco. Remove bay leaf and discard.

9. To serve, mound rice in pre-heated gumbo bowls; ladle some gumbo over the rice; garnish with parsley and green onion tops. Each serving should include shrimp, oyster and ham.

10. Offer filé at the table.

Bea Weber
Abbeville, La.

1 pint of oysters, with liquid

1/2 cup of finely chopped parsley

1/2 cup of finely chopped green onion tops

6 drops of Tabasco

Filé powder

Shrimp-Tasso Gumbo

2 pounds of tasso

3 pounds of fresh heads-on shrimp
(or 2 pounds of frozen tails)

3 tablespoons of lard or bacon
drippings

3 tablespoons of flour

2 large onions, chopped

1 bellpepper, chopped

4 cloves of garlic, minced

3 pounds of fresh okra, sliced
(or 4 packages of frozen)

1 32-ounce can of tomatoes

1/4 teaspoon of cayenne (or more)

Salt and freshly ground black
pepper, to taste

The Cajuns have a type of dried beef called tasso that's a cousin to the pemmican of the Indians and the jerky beef of Western frontiersmen. Rubbed with salt and spices before being dried, it has a pungent flavor and makes a delicious gumbo when combined with shrimp and okra. It is sold in neighborhood groceries throughout the Acadian country of south Louisiana. In other areas jerky dried beef or corned beef can be used as a substitute.

1. Cover the tasso chunks with water and soak them overnight. Drain. Cover the tasso with fresh water and boil gently for two hours, or until it is soft and tender. Take it out, dice it, and set it aside.

2. Cover the shrimp with the water the tasso was boiled in, and boil for five minutes. Remove the shrimp, peel, and set aside. The stock in the pot may be too strong and salty for use as gumbo stock, so taste it and dilute with fresh water until it's palatable.

3. Melt the lard in a large skillet, add the flour, and make a brown roux. Add the onion, bellpepper, and garlic to the roux, and cook until the vegetables are wilted.

4. Add the sliced okra to the skillet and continue cooking until the okra loses its gummy consistency.

5. Chop the tomatoes and add them to the skillet. Cook a little longer, add the cayenne and black pepper, and stir well.

6. Place this mixture in a stew pot, and add the tasso and shrimp and enough tasso-shrimp stock to cover by one inch. If necessary, add water.

7. Cook at a slow boil for 45 minutes more. Add salt if necessary.

8. Ladle over rice in preheated soup bowls.

Serves eight.

Howard Mitcham
Creole Gumbo And All That Jazz

Shrimp & Sausage Gumbo

1/2 cup of flour

1/4 cup of cooking oil

1 large onion, chopped

1/2 cup of cubed salt meat

1 cup and 1 quart of water

1 cup of smoked sausage,
cut into one-inch pieces

3 cups of peeled raw shrimp

Parsley and onion tops, chopped

1/4 teaspoon of filé

Rice

1. Make a brown roux of the flour and oil.

2. Add onion and salt meat; cook until dark brown, about 20 minutes.

3. Add one cup of water and the smoked sausage; cook about 20 minutes, stirring occasionally.

4. Add shrimp; cover, then cook another 20 minutes, stirring occasionally.

5. Add parsley and onion tops.

6. Add one quart of water and bring to a boil; stir, cover and reduce heat; cook on low heat for 30 minutes. Add another cup or more of water to thin out gumbo, if desired.

7. Turn off the heat and add filé.

8. Serve over rice.

Mrs. Gloria Cheramie
Lafourche Parish, La.

Salmon Gumbo

For Catholics living in predominantly Catholic south Louisiana prior to the 1970s, Friday was always a day of abstinence from eating meat. So, in the spirit of sacrifice, and compliance with the church's rule, many a meatless dish was concocted, including Salmon Gumbo. While salmon was not found in the waters of this region, canned salmon was found on the grocers' shelves. Salmon Gumbo thus became a commonplace Friday meal, being economical, tasty and easily adaptable to recipes already being used in the region.

4 tablespoons of roux

1/2 cup of chopped onion

1/2 cup of chopped celery

1 8-ounce can of stewed tomatoes

2 1/2 quarts of water

Salt and pepper, to taste

1 15 1/2-ounce can of salmon

4 raw eggs, unbeaten

1. Place roux, onion and celery in a four-quart pot. Cook over medium heat until vegetables are tender.

2. Add stewed tomatoes, water and seasonings. Bring to a boil.

3. Add salmon and eggs. Don't stir.

4. Lower heat. Cover pot and cook 30 minutes.

6. Serve with hot rice.

Debby Simon
Kaplan, La.

Oyster Filé Gumbo

1/2 cup of bacon drippings

1/4 cup of flour

1 cup of diced celery

1/2 cup of chopped bellpepper

1 cup of chopped onion

Salt and pepper, to taste

1 quart of water

36 freshly shucked or frozen oysters, with liquid

1 teaspoon of filé

Cooked rice

1. Heat bacon drippings over medium heat in Dutch oven or large, heavy saucepan. Stir-in flour to make roux.

2. Add celery, bellpepper, onion, salt and pepper. Sauté, then add the water, cover and simmer over low heat for 15 minutes.

3. Stir-in oysters. Simmer over low heat just until edges of oysters begin to curl.

4. Remove from heat. Stir-in filé.

5. Serve with rice.

Serves four to six.

Mabel Kirby
The General Federation Of Women's Clubs Cookbook: *America Cooks*

Oyster Gumbo A La Antoine

This is a bit of haute cuisine. Antoine's Restaurant of New Orleans would never give anyone their recipe for Oysters Rockefeller, but in 1962 Roy Alciatore (now deceased) gave me his recipe for Oyster Gumbo. Like all great recipes, it's very simple and easy to prepare.

1. Make a good roux with the flour and butter by allowing it to brown (but not burn) while stirring constantly over a low flame.

2. To the brown roux add the crabs.

3. Stir and cook a little, and then add the bay leaves and the thyme.

4. Add the raw sliced okra and allow to cook awhile. Add the tomatoes and allow to cook some more.

5. Next add a quart each of oyster liquid and water at the same time.

6. Season with salt and pepper. Allow the gumbo to simmer for an hour and a half.

7. Ten minutes before serving, add the shrimp and the raw oysters.

8. Serve with cooked rice.

Antoine's Restaurant
New Orleans, La.
as reported by Howard Mitcham
in *Creole Gumbo And All That Jazz*

3 tablespoons of flour

5 tablespoons of butter

6 raw hard-shell crabs, cut in pieces

2 bay leaves

1 teaspoon of thyme

1 pound of raw okra, sliced

6 raw tomatoes with skins removed and chopped fine

1 quart of oyster liquid

1 quart of water

Salt and pepper, to taste

1 pound of peeled raw shrimp

5 dozen raw oysters

Opelousas Oyster Gumbo

1/4 cup of all-purpose flour

1/4 cup of butter or margarine

1 cup of chopped bellpepper

1 cup of chopped onion

1 clove of garlic, crushed

2 cups of water

2 tablespoons of snipped fresh parsley

1 teaspoon of salt

1/4 teaspoon each of ground black pepper and dried thyme

Dash of ground red pepper

1 bay leaf

1/2 pound of peeled, deveined raw shrimp

1 pint of oysters with liquid

Gumbo filé*

3 cups of hot cooked rice

1. Brown flour in butter until it is a deep red-brown, stirring constantly to prevent burning.

2. Add bellpeppers, onion, and garlic. Cook until vegetables are tender.

3. Stir-in water, parsley and seasonings. Cook slowly for 30 minutes.

4. Add shrimp and oysters with liquid. Bring to a boil and cook five minutes longer, until shrimp are pink and oysters begin to curl.

5. Remove from heat and add gumbo filé, to taste.

Serve in shallow bowls over fluffy rice.

Makes six servings.

* Never add filé while gumbo is cooking, because boiling after filé is added tends to make gumbo stringy.

USA Rice Council

164

Scallop & Catfish Gumbo

1. Make roux by heating oil and gradually adding flour. Stir constantly until dark golden brown.

2. Add onion and sauté until wilted.

3. Add two cups of warm water. Bring to a boil. Keep on a high simmer for 45 minutes.

4. Add one bottle of clam juice, three cups of Seafood Stock, scallops and catfish. Cook for 15 minutes.

5. Taste for seasoning. Add salt and cayenne as needed.

6. Serve over hot cooked rice.

Makes six servings or 12 appetizers.

Bea Weber
Abbeville, La.

1/4 cup of oil

1/4 cup of flour

1 large onion, chopped

2 cups of warm water

1 bottle of clam juice

3 cups of Seafood Stock (See Seafood Stock recipe, page 40)

1 pound of scallops, seasoned with salt and cayenne

1/2 pound of catfish, cut in nugget sizes and seasoned with salt and cayenne

Hot cooked rice

Crab Gumbo

3 pounds of fresh or frozen shrimp

3 dozen large, live crabs
(or 3 pounds of frozen crabmeat)

3 tablespoons of butter

3 tablespoons of flour

2 large onions, chopped

1 bellpepper, chopped

3 cloves of garlic, minced

2 pounds of fresh okra, sliced
(or 3 packages of frozen)

1/4 cup of chopped parsley

2 bay leaves

1/2 teaspoon of thyme

1/4 teaspoon of cayenne

1/2 teaspoon of freshly ground
black pepper

5 Creole tomatoes, peeled and
chopped (or a 32-ounce can)

Salt, to taste

1. Peel the shrimp and set aside. It is not necessary to devein them. Reserve the heads and shells.

2. Wash the live crabs thoroughly in the sink. (They'll protest vigorously, but ignore them.)

3. Place crabs in a large pot, cover with boiling water, and add a little salt. After the water returns to a boil, cook the crabs for 20 minutes.

4. Remove the crabs and place them in the sink to cool. Save the stock in the pot.

5. Crush the shrimp shells and heads with a pestle or a bottle in a flat-bottomed pan. Add this mixture to the stock in the pot.

6. Remove the crab claws and set aside. Remove the top shells of the crabs, scrape all the crab fat out of the corners of the shells and save it. Twist off the legs and fins. Crush the top shells and the legs and fins and add them to the stock pot. Boil all these shells vigorously for 30 minutes, and then strain off the liquid through a triple layer of cheesecloth. (This makes a beautiful stock for your gumbo.)

7. In a large, heavy skillet melt the butter, add the flour and cook, stirring constantly to make a roux.

8. To the roux add the onion, bellpepper and garlic, and cook until the vegetables are soft and transparent. Add more butter if necessary.

9. Add the okra and cook it until it loses its gummy consistency and is smooth.

10. Add the crab fat, parsley, bay leaves, thyme, cayenne and black pepper to the skillet and stir them in, cooking a little longer.

11. Put the vegetables in a large stew pot and add the tomatoes.

12. Crack the crab claws and put them in.

13. Clean off the crabs by removing and discarding the gills, the mouth part, the small bag next to it at the front, and the "apron" on the bottom. Clean out the body cavity and save all the fat, the yellow liver, and any red coral (eggs) that may be present. Add all this–the "caviar" of the crab–to the pot. Discard the intestine, the white stringy thing in the body cavity.

14. Break the crab bodies into halves, cut each half into two or three pieces, and add to the stew pot.

15. Add enough of the strained stock to the stew pot to cover all contents by one inch. If more liquid is necessary, add fish stock or bouillon.

16. Simmer for an hour, add the shrimp, cook for a half hour more, and at the end add salt carefully. The gumbo should be salty and savory.

17. Preheat soup bowls, place a little steamed rice in the bottom of each, and ladle the gumbo over the rice. Serve piping hot with hot french bread.

Serves eight to 10.

Howard Mitcham
Creole Gumbo And All That Jazz

Crab-Hominy Gumbo

2 dozen large, live crabs
(or 2 pounds of frozen crabmeat)

3 tablespoons of lard or shortening

2 tablespoons of flour

2 large onions, chopped

3 cloves of garlic, minced

2 pounds of fresh okra,
cut in 1/2-inch slices

1 12-ounce can of hominy

1 16-ounce can of tomatoes,
drained and chopped

4 tablespoons of chopped parsley

1/4 teaspoon of cayenne

1/2 teaspoon of freshly ground
black pepper

Salt, to taste

1. Wash the live crabs thoroughly in the sink.

2. Place them in a large pot and cover with boiling water. After the water comes to a boil, cook the crabs for 20 minutes.

3. Remove and cool them. Reserve the water.

4. Twist off the crab claws, legs and flippers, and set them aside. Remove the top shells of the crabs, and scrape off the spongy gills. Clean out all the crab fat in the corners of the shells and reserve it. Also save all the crab fat and yellow liver from the crab's body cavity. Break off the mouth part and remove the "apron" from the body.

5. Break the body into two halves and pick out all the meat. Crack the crab claws and pick out this meat. (This picking is a tedious chore, but it's worth the bother. You should get about two pounds of meat and crab fat.)

6. Place the crab shells, legs and flippers in a flat-bottomed pot, and crush them with a pestle or a heavy bottle. Cover with part of the water in which the crabs were boiled. Boil vigorously for 30 minutes to extract the essences. Strain the liquid, set it aside, and discard the shells.

7. In a large pot or Dutch oven (aluminum or stainless steel preferred to iron, which turns okra black) heat the lard and add the flour to make a roux.

8. Add the onion and garlic and cook until transparent.

9. Add the okra and cook until it loses its gummy consistency.

10. Add the hominy, tomatoes with their juice, parsley, cayenne, black pepper, and a tablespoon of salt.

11. Cover the ingredients in the pot by about an inch with the crab water, the juice from the shells, and the crab fat.

12. Simmer for an hour.

13. Add the crab meat, and then simmer for a half hour more. At the end adjust the salt. (The gumbo should be salty and savory, hot and peppery, and thick.)

14. Serve gumbo in preheated soup bowls over mounds of cooked rice.

Serves six to eight

Howard Mitcham
Creole Gumbo And All That Jazz

Crawfish Gumbo

2 cups of flour

1 1/2 cups of cooking oil

1 large onion, chopped

3 gallons of hot water

1 cup of chopped celery

2 chicken breasts (preferably stewing hen), cut into small pieces

2 pounds of crawfish tails

Salt, cayenne and black pepper

1 cup of chopped onion tops

1/2 cup of chopped parsley

(First Place Winner: Louisiana-Texas Crawfish Cooking Competition, 1990)

1. Make roux by mixing flour and oil in heavy iron pot and cooking until dark brown.

2. Just before roux burns, add chopped onion to quench heat and keep roux from burning. Take roux off heat and sauté onion.

3. Mix with three gallons of hot water.

4. Add celery, chicken, half a pound of crawfish (chopped fine and seasoned with salt, black pepper and cayenne pepper.)

5. Boil gently at least two hours.

6. Fifteen minutes before serving, add one and a half pounds of crawfish, onion tops and parsley.

René Hebert
Originally from Kaplan, La.; now residing in Alvin, Tex.

Crawfish Filé Gumbo

1. In heavy pot make a roux by adding flour to heated oil; cook over medium heat, stirring constantly until deep golden brown.

2. Take pot off fire; add onion, garlic and celery. Stir and cook until soft, four to five minutes.

3. Add tomatoes and cook five minutes longer.

4. Add fat and water. Stir until it comes to a hard boil. Reduce heat to simmer.

5. Season with salt and pepper.

6. Cover and cook 30 to 45 minutes.

7. In a small saucepan cook butter, parsley, green onion and tails for two or three minutes, then add to gumbo.

8. Serve in soup bowls with hot cooked rice and use half a teaspoon of filé per serving.

"Cajun Creole Cookery"
The Daily Iberian

1/4 cup of all-purpose flour

1/4 cup of cooking oil

1 medium onion, chopped

1 clove of garlic, minced

1 stalk of celery, chopped

1 cup of whole tomatoes (fresh or canned), chopped

Crawfish fat and water to make 4 pints

Salt and pepper, to taste

2 tablespoons of butter or margarine

1 tablespoon each of chopped parsley and green onion tops

1 1/2 cups of crawfish tails

Gumbo filé

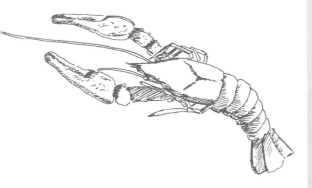

Catfish Gumbo

1 pound of skinned catfish fillets or other skinned fish fillets, fresh or frozen, cut into 1-inch pieces

1/2 cup of chopped celery

1/2 cup of chopped bellpepper

1/2 cup of chopped onion

1 clove of garlic, finely chopped

1/4 cup of melted fat or oil

2 beef bouillon cubes

2 cups of boiling water

1 can (1 lb.) of tomatoes

1 package (10 ozs.) of frozen okra, sliced

2 teaspoons of salt

1/4 teaspoon of pepper

1/4 teaspoon of thyme

1 whole bay leaf

Dash of liquid hot pepper sauce

1 1/2 cups of hot cooked rice

1. Thaw frozen fillets. Cut into one-inch pieces.

2. Cook celery, bellpepper, onion and garlic in fat until tender.

3. Dissolve bouillon cubes in water. Add bouillon, tomatoes, okra and seasonings. Cover and simmer for 30 minutes.

4. Add fish. Cover and simmer for 15 minutes longer or until fish flakes easily when tested with a fork.

5. Remove bay leaf.

6. Place a quarter cup of rice in each of six soup bowls. Fill with gumbo.

Serves six.

"Cajun Creole Cookery"
The Daily Iberian

VEGETABLE

Cabbage Gumbo

1 large head of cabbage (green and white mixed)

1 tablespoon of shortening

1 round steak, cut in bite-size pieces

2 large slices of lean ham, cut in bite-size pieces

1 large onion, chopped

2 pounds of Creole sausage, cut into 1-inch slices

1 pod of red pepper, without the seeds

Salt, black pepper and cayenne, to taste

1 pint of milk

2 tablespoons of flour

1. Separate the cabbage into leaves and wash each leaf separately and thoroughly. Chop the entire head very fine.

2. Heat the shortening in a deep, heavy pot until hot; add the beef and ham.

3. When the meat begins to brown, add the onion and the sausage; add the chopped cabbage, stirring and pouring in enough water to prevent it from burning.

4. Add the red pepper pod, a dash of cayenne, salt and black pepper, to taste.

5. Allow the ingredients to cook well, gradually adding, if necessary, a little water, and stirring frequently to prevent burning.

6. When thoroughly cooked, add cream sauce made from one pint of milk and two tablespoons of flour mixed thoroughly, so as not to be lumpy.

7. Stir this into the gumbo while boiling, and continue stirring for five minutes.

8. Serve with cooked rice.

Note: The gumbo must not be allowed to stand on the heat after the flour has been boiled in it for five minutes, as it may burn.

The Times-Picayune
The Picayune Original Creole Cookbook

Gumbo Vert

1. In a large gumbo pot, make a dark roux with the butter and flour.

2. Add remaining ingredients except for salt, pepper and filé.

3. Add enough water to bring level about two-thirds to top of ingredients.

4. Bring to a boil and then simmer slowly for at least 30 minutes. Add more water if needed.

5. Add salt and pepper to taste and simmer another 30 minutes.

6. Shortly before serving, add filé and serve over rice.

Fran Stallings
Cajun Accent: A Collection of Recipes in the Acadian Tradition

1 stick of butter

1/2 cup of flour

1 large or 2 medium turnip roots, diced

1 large or 2 medium potatoes, diced

1 large onion or 4 green onions, chopped

1/2 cup of chopped celery

1 bellpepper, chopped

1 hot pepper or jalapeno, chopped

2 cups of finely chopped turnip greens

1 clove of elephant garlic, chopped

3 cloves of regular garlic, chopped

4 large links of smoked sausage, sliced into 1-inch pieces

10 large sprigs of parsley, chopped

3 bay leaves

Salt and black pepper

One tablespoon of filé

Gumbo Z'Herbes

10 ounces of fresh spinach or 1 10-oz. package of frozen leaf spinach, thawed

10 ounces of fresh mustard greens or 1 10-oz. package of frozen mustard greens, thawed

10 ounces of fresh turnip greens or 1 10-oz. package of frozen turnip greens, thawed

10 ounces of fresh collard greens or 1 10-oz. package of frozen collard greens, thawed

1/2 medium cabbage, shredded

2 bay leaves, minced

1 teaspoon each of dried leaf basil, dried leaf thyme and dried leaf oregano

1/4 teaspoon of ground allspice

1/8 teaspoon of ground cloves

1/4 teaspoon of freshly grated nutmeg

4 quarts of Louisiana Brown Poultry Stock (See recipe, page 38.) or canned chicken stock

Seasoning Mix (Recipe follows)

1 pound of lean boneless pork, cut into bite-sized pieces

1 pound of smoked ham, cut into bite-sized pieces

Gumbo Z'Herbes is often referred to as the king of gumbos in New Orleans. In predominantly Catholic south Louisiana, it was traditionally served on Good Friday. The logic was that, after so many days of Lenten abstinence and fasting, the body needed the sort of revitalization provided by a combination of greens. The old Creole women would rise early in the morning on Good Friday and head for the Vieux Carre's French Market to buy their greens for the day's Gumbo Z'Herbes. The vendors would have their bright, crisp greens temptingly displayed. Stalls would be filled with the cries of "Get your twelve greens, lady," or "Get your seven greens, madame." Legend had it—and it is still nice to believe—that for every green added to the Gumbo Z'Herbes on this day, a new friend would be made during the following year!

1. Wash fresh greens; tear into small pieces. Remove large stalks and ribs.

2. Place cleaned or frozen greens, cabbage, bay leaves, basil, thyme, oregano, allspice, cloves and nutmeg into a large soup pot.

3. Add stock and enough water to cover greens by three inches.

4. Bring to a boil. Reduce heat. Cover; simmer while preparing remaining ingredients.

5. Prepare Seasoning Mix. Add pork and ham to Seasoning Mix. Shake to coat lightly. Set seasoned meat aside while oil heats.

6. Heat oil in a large, heavy skillet over medium-high heat. When oil is very hot, add seasoned meat; stir until brown on all sides. Remove browned meat with a slotted spoon; add to simmering greens; reduce heat to medium.

7. Add onions, celery, bellpepper and garlic to skillet. Cook until vegetables are wilted, about five minutes. Remove vegetables with a slotted spoon; add to simmering greens.

8. Stir-in sugar; simmer, uncovered, one hour.

9. Season with salt, black pepper and cayenne. Cover; simmer for two hours.

10. About 10 minutes before serving, gently stir-in oysters with their liquid, green onions and parsley. Cook until edges of oysters curl.

(Continued on next page)

2/3 cup of vegetable oil
2 large onions, chopped
4 celery stalks, chopped
1 large bellpepper, chopped
4 large garlic cloves, chopped
2 tablespoons of sugar
Salt, to taste
Freshly ground black pepper
Cayenne pepper, to taste
24 shucked oysters with liquid (about 2 pints)
12 green onions, thinly sliced
1/2 cup of minced fresh parsley
3 1/2 tablespoons of filé
5 cups of hot cooked rice

1/2 teaspoon each of salt, freshly ground black pepper, cayenne pepper, paprika, onion powder and garlic powder

11. Spoon about half a cup of rice into each soup bowl. Spoon gumbo over rice; top with a pinch of filé powder.

Makes 8 to 10 servings.

SEASONING MIX

1. Place all ingredients in a large plastic bag.

2. Shake to combine.

Terry Thompson
Cajun-Creole Cooking

Fresh Okra, Dried Shrimp & Crabmeat Gumbo

1. Smother okra in margarine by slowly turning it over and over with large spoon on a low heat.

2. Add tomatoes, onion, bellpepper and garlic. Add a small amount of water at a time for about 45 minutes.

3. After okra and vegetables are smothered together add a dash of Kitchen Bouquet for desired color.

4. Add the cream of celery soup and water (five quarts).

5. Stir-in the dried shrimp and the water the shrimp was soaked in.

6. Add the crabmeat.

7. Season, to taste. Cook on low fire for 45 minutes.

Wade Byrd
The Official Louisiana Seafood & Wild Game Cookbook

3 to 4 pounds of okra, cut up

3 tablespoons of margarine

2 tomatoes, cut into wedges

2 onions, chopped fine

3/4 bellpepper, cut up

1 pod of garlic, chopped

Kitchen Bouquet

1 can of cream of celery soup

5 quarts of water

1/2 pound of dried shrimp, soaked for 1/2 hour in 1 1/2 cups of hot water

1 pound of crabmeat

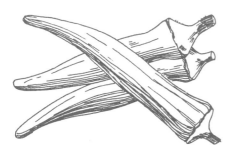

Quick Louisiana Gumbo

1 cup of chopped onion

2 tablespoons of bacon drippings, butter, or margarine

1 28-ounce can of peeled whole tomatoes, chopped

1 1/2 teaspoons of salt

1/2 teaspoon of crushed red pepper

1 10-ounce package of frozen cut okra

1 quart of chicken broth

1 pound of fish fillets, cut in large pieces

3 cups of hot cooked rice

1. Cook onion in bacon drippings in large skillet until soft but not brown.

2. Add tomatoes, salt, and red pepper.

3. Bring to a boil, reduce heat, cover, and simmer 15 minutes.

4. Remove cover; add okra and broth; continue cooking 15 minutes.

5. Add fish and cook 10 minutes longer.

6. Serve in individual soup plates with hot rice.

Makes eight servings.

USA Rice Council

Tasso-Okra Gumbo

1. Put tasso in a pot with enough water to cover.

2. When it starts to boil, reduce heat to medium and cook for an hour to an hour and a half. Add more water if it boils down too much, and cook longer if it doesn't test tender when pricked with a fork.

3. Select a thick aluminum pot. (Do not use an iron pot to cook okra). Put in the shortening; when hot, reduce to medium and add okra. Cover to cook, removing cover often to stir in order to keep it from scorching.

4. When sticky substance has disappeared completely and okra is brownish in color, add the onion, bellpepper and garlic and season lightly.

5. After the onion and bellpepper have wilted, add the tomatoes and their liquid.

6. Chop the tasso into small pieces and add to okra along with a cupful of the liquid used to cook the tasso. Add more water and cook over medium heat for 30 to 45 minutes, stirring occasionally.

7. When done, taste for seasoning and add more if necessary. If okra cooks down too much, add more water and cook five minutes more.

Edley Dupre
Quelque Chose Beaucoup Bon

1 pound of tasso

Water

2 tablespoons of shortening

2 pounds of okra, cut into 1/4-inch slices

1 medium onion, chopped fine

1 medium bellpepper, chopped

2 cloves of garlic, minced

Salt, black pepper and red pepper

1 can of whole tomatoes

Gumbo Creole
(Okra-Seafood Gumbo)

3 pounds of okra, cut fine

4 tablespoons of oil

1/3 cup of peanut oil

1/3 cup of flour

4 medium onions, chopped

4 teaspoons of tomato paste

4 cups of water

2 pounds of shrimp

1 pint of oysters

1 pound of crabmeat

1 cup of ham, diced (optional)

3/4 cup of chopped parsley

2 cloves of garlic, chopped

3 bay leaves

1 cup of chopped celery

Salt and pepper

Tabasco sauce

Cooked rice

This gumbo recipe is a very old family favorite that goes back to my great-grandmother. It is also one of the favorites of students in my cooking classes. It was included by Mrs. Lillian Marshall in her book for Southern Living titled Cooking Across The South.

1. Sauté okra in four tablespoons of oil until thick. Set aside.

2. Make a dark roux with peanut oil and flour.

3. Add onions and tomato paste.

4. Add water and blend well.

5. Add okra, shrimp, oysters, crab and ham.

6. Season with parsley, garlic, bay leaves, celery, salt and pepper.

7. Simmer uncovered about one hour.

8. Add Tabasco, to taste. Serve in soup bowls over cooked rice.

Chef Earl Peyroux
Gourmet Cooking by Earl Peyroux

Creole Okra Gumbo

1. Cook crabs in boiling water until shells turn red.

2. Remove from water, crack claws and remove meat.

3. Remove shell from crabs, break breast into quarters and throw away soft and spongy part. Put broken shells in three cups of water.

4. Prepare fresh shrimp the same way.

5. Save shrimp shells after meat has been removed and add them to crab shells. Simmer shells in covered pot about one hour.

6. Heat lard, add flour and combine. Turn heat down to low, add onion, garlic and tomato paste.

7. Add okra to tomato mixture. If fresh okra is used, cook the mixture 30 minutes; if canned okra, cook 10 minutes.

8. Add water drained from crab and shrimp shells and cook 15 minutes. Throw shells away.

9. Add shrimp, crab, parsley, bay leaf, thyme, salt and pepper.

10. Simmer for two hours, stirring occasionally. Serve over hot rice.

Mrs. James F. (Annie) Barnes
Formerly of Jeanerette, La.; now of E. Pittsburgh, Penn.

3 crabs

1 pound of fresh shrimp

3 tablespoons of lard

1 tablespoon of flour

1 tablespoon of minced onion

1 clove of minced garlic

1 tablespoon of tomato paste

1 can of okra or 1 pound of fresh okra, cut in one-inch pieces

1 tablespoon of parsley

1 bay leaf

1 sprig of thyme

Salt and pepper, to taste

Credits

The authors and publisher of this book gratefully acknowledge the contributions made by the individuals and publishers who provided recipes and/or information relative to the history, evolution and preparation of gumboes. The page(s) upon which their material appears in this book is shown in parentheses at the end of the respective entries below.

Allain, Mathé Dr. A Presentation, "Louisiana Cajun And Creole Cuisine," 1992 Annual Meeting of The Attakapas Historical Association, Lafayette, La., January 25, 1992 (pp. 12, 13)

Antoine's Restaurant, New Orleans, La. (p. 163)

Barnes, Mrs. James F. (Annie). Formerly of Jeanerette, La., now residing in E. Pittsburgh, Pa. "Cajun-Creole Cookery," supplement to *The Daily Iberian*, Sept. 1981 (p. 183)

Barton, Debby Maugans, "Make-Ahead Roux For Quick Cajun Cooking," *Creative Ideas For Living* (810 Seventh Ave., New York, NY 10019), 16:72, September, 1985 (p. 76) Copyright © 1985, 1986. PSC Limited Partnership (p. 23, 72, 73)

Beaullieu, Mrs. Elton, Jeanerette, La. "Cajun-Creole Cookery," supplement to *The Daily Iberian*, September, 1981 (p. 89)

Bienvenu, Marcelle, "Bonne Cuisine. Gumbo & Potatoes," *The Kaplan Herald*, Copyright © January 3, 1990 (pp. 68, 69)

Bourque, Bryan R. Black's Oyster Bar, Abbeville, La. (pp.132)

Broussard, Mrs. Marie B., Kaplan, La. (p. 46)

Broussard, Marie L., Kaplan, La. (p. 65)

Bunetta, Teresa Hicks. *Acadiana French And American Cuisine Seasoned With His Love*. Lafayette, La.: Gospel Outreach Publishers, Inc., Copyright © 1977 (p. 26)

Byrd, Wade (Editor). *The Official Louisiana Seafood & Wild Game Cookbook*. Baton Rouge: Louisiana Department of Wildlife and Fisheries, Copyright © 1985 (p. 179)

Cahn, Joe. The New Orleans School Of Cooking, New Orleans, La. (pp. 64, 115)

"Cajun-Creole Cookery," Supplement to *The Daily Iberian*, New Iberia, La. (p. 87, 88, 90, 91, 104, 106, 107, 108, 122, 171, 172)

Cheramie, Mrs. Gloria. Lafourche Parish, La. Recipe printed in *Acadiana Profile's Cajun Cooking, Part 2*. Lafayette, La.: Acadian News Agency, Inc. © 1987 (p. 160)

Citizen, Emelda, Lafayette, La. (p. 84)

Clark, Morton G. *French-American Cooking From New Orleans To Quebec*. New York: Harper & Row Publishers Inc., 1967 (pp. 11, 12, 138)

Creole Cookery Book (New Orleans: The Christian Women's Exchange, 1885 (p. 10)

Doiron, Jeanette Pennell (Editor). *Food, Glorious Food*. Beaumont, Tex.: The Woman's Club, second printing, Copyright © October 1983 (p. 45)

Don's Seafood Hut, Lafayette, La. (p. 114)

Dupre, Edley. Recipe printed in Mercedes Vidrine's *Quelque Chose Beaucoup Bon* (Recipes from Cajun Kitchens). Baton Rouge, La.: Claitor's Publishing Division, Phone: (504) 344-0476. Copyright © 1973 (p. 181)

Dupre, Rena. Recipe printed in Mercedes Vidrine's *Quelque Chose Beaucoup Bon* (Recipes from Cajun Kitchens). Baton Rouge, La.: Claitor's Publishing Division, Phone: (504) 344-0476. Copyright © 1973 (p. 109)

Foreman, Mrs. Virgie B. Rayne, La. "13th Annual Cookbook," *The Daily Advertiser*, June 26, 1975 (p. 79)

Graugnard, Mrs. Bertha. St. James Parish, La. Recipe printed in *Foods A La Louisiane*. Baton Rouge: Louisiana Farm Bureau Women, Copyright © 1985 (p. 152)

Gourmet Magazine, February 1957. (p. 100)

Griffin, Mrs. G.W., Cataline Hotel, Pass Christian, Miss., "Cajun-Creole Cookery," *The Daily Iberian*, Sept. 23, 1961 (p. 101)

Guidry, Lena. Sweetlake, Calcasieu Parish, La. Recipe printed in "Gumbos That Warm The Heart On A Wet Winter Night," *Acadiana Profile*, Fourth Quarter 1987 (p. 153)

Guidry, Mrs. Oris. Recipe printed in Mercedes Vidrine's *Quelque Chose Beaucoup Bon* (Recipes from Cajun Kitchens). Baton Rouge, La.: Claitor's Publishing Division, Phone: (504) 344-0476. Copyright © 1973 (p. 50)

Hanchey, Louise. "How We Cooked: Some Old Louisiana Recipes." Lafayette, La.: Lafayette Natural History Museum and Planetarium, 1976 (p. 10)

Hearn, Lafcadio. *La Cuisine Creole* (1885); reprinted in New Orleans: Pelican Publishing Company, Inc., 1967 (p. 10)

Hebert, Mrs. Gertrude. Olivier, La., "Cajun Creole Cookery," *The Daily Iberian*, Sept. 1981 (p. 78)

Hebert, Mrs. Nedia B. Jeanerette, La., "Cajun Creole Cookery, *The Daily Iberian*, September 1981 (p. 60)

Hebert, René. Originally from Kaplan, La., now residing in Alvin, Tex. (p. 170)

James And Sudwischer. *Cajun Christmas Creations*. Crowley, La.: James and Sudwischer, Copyright © 1986 (p. 61, 92, 93)

Kirby, Mabel. Recipe printed in *The General Federation of Women's Clubs Cookbook: America Cooks*. New York: G.P. Putnam's Sons, Copyright © 1967 (p.162)

Land, Mary. *Mary Land's Louisiana Cookery*. Baton Rouge: Louisiana State University Press, Copyright © 1954 (p.97, 126)

Landry, Jeanne H. *Sauté: A Collection of Creole Recipes For The Microwave Oven*. New Orleans: Jeanne H. Landry, 1977 (pp. 29, 125, 139)

Louisiana Farm Bureau Women. *Foods A La Louisiane*. Baton Rouge: Louisiana Farm Bureau Women, Copyright © 1985 (p. 28)

Maras, Gerard. Mr. B's Bistro, New Orleans, La. (p. 56)

The McIlhenny Company, *From The Land of Tabasco® Sauce*, Avery Island, La.: The McIlhenny Company, Copyright © 1984 (p. 121)

McKee, Gwen. *The Little Gumbo Book*. Baton Rouge: Quail Ridge Press, Inc., Copyright © Third Printing, October 1989 (p. 49, 127, 128, 131)

Miller, Mrs. Ira. Recipe printed in Mercedes Vidrine's *Quelque Chose Beaucoup Bon* (Recipes from Cajun Kitchens). Baton Rouge, La.: Claitor's Publishing Division, Phone: (504) 344-0476. Copyright © 1973 (p. 27)

Mitcham, Howard. *Creole Gumbo And All That Jazz*, © 1978 by Howard Mitcham. Reprinted with permission of Addison Wesley Publishing Co., Inc., Reading, Mass. (pp. 13, 14, 16, 18, 19, 20, 136, 137, 140, 141, 142, 143, 158, 159, 163, 166, 167, 168, 169)

Montegut, Mrs. Lester. St. Martinville, La. "Cajun-Creole Cookery," Supplement to *The Daily Iberian*, September 18, 1954 (p. 74)

Morgan, J.D. Recipe printed in *Pots, Pans And Pioneers I*. Lenexa, Kan.: Cookbook Publishers, Inc., Copyright © 1976 (p. 59)

Nichols, Nell B. (editor) *America's Best Vegetable Recipes*. Garden City, N.Y.: Doubleday & Company, Copyright © 1970 by *Farm Journal* (p. 123)

Payne, Susan, "Cooking In The Cajun Style," Reprinted from *Creative Ideas For Living* (810 Seventh Ave., New York, NY 10019), 15:65, October 1984, Copyright © 1985, 1986. PSC Limited Partnership (pp. 129, 130)

Perrin, Albert. Kaplan, La. (p. 70)

Pettey, Mrs. William. Recipe printed in *The Gulf Gourmet Presents Selected Recipes From The Mississippi Coast*. Gulfport, Miss.: Westminster Academy Mothers Club of Gulfport, Miss., Copyright © 1983 (p. 144)

Peyroux, Earl. *Gourmet Cooking By Earl Peyroux*. Pensacola, Fla.: Earl Peyroux. Copyright © 1982 (pp. 17, 18, 103, 148, 149, 182)

Poret, Mrs. George C. Recipe printed in *The General Federation Of Women's Clubs Cookbook: America Cooks*. New York: G.P. Putnam's Sons, Copyright © 1967 (p. 76)

Potts, Bobby. *Louisiana And Mississippi Plantation Cookbook*. New Orleans: Express Publishing Co. (p. 105)

Prudhomme, Paul. "Authentic Cajun Cooking: Recipes by Chef Paul Prudhomme," *Acadiana Profile*, Copyright © Fourth Quarter 1985 (pp. 154)

Prudhomme, Paul. "Seven Steak, Tasso And Okra Gumbo," "Cajun-Creole Cookery," Supplement to *The Daily Iberian*, September, 1985 (pp. 42)

Pryolo, Mrs. Mary. Lafourche Parish, La. Recipe printed in "Cajun Cooking, Part II,": *Acadiana Profile*, December, 1977 (p. 147)

Robin, C.C. *Voyage To Louisiana, 1803-1805*. New Orleans: Pelican Publishing Company, 1966 (p. 10)

Stallings, Fran. Recipe printed in *Cajun Accent, A Collection of Recipes in the Acadian Tradition*. Lafayette, La.: Cajun Classic Press, Inc., 1979 (p. 175)

Stamps, Louise C. Recipe printed in *The General Federation Of Women's Clubs Cookbook: America Cooks*. New York: G.P. Putnam's Sons, Copyright © 1967 (pp. 134, 135)

Thompson, Terry. Reproduced from *Cajun-Creole Cooking*, published by HP Books, a division of Price Stern Sloan, Los Angeles, Calif. Copyright © 1986 (pp. 10, 11, 20, 24, 25, 36, 37, 38, 39, 40, 62, 63, 94, 95, 96, 118, 119, 176, 177, 178)

The Times-Picayune. "The Picayune Original Creole Cookbook." New Orleans: The Times-Picayune Publishing Co., Copyright © 1966 (pp. 110, 111, 145, 174)

Trahan, Catherine. Kaplan, La. (p.75)

USA Rice Council Home Economics Department. Statement given in written communication. Houston: April, 1990 (p. 32, 52, 58, 86, 124, 146, 164, 180)

Weber, Beatrice. Abbeville, La. (pp. 22, 33, 44, 47, 48, 53, 54, 55, 66, 67, 71, 77, 80, 81, 82, 83, 98, 99, 120, 150, 151, 156, 157, 165)

Webster's Ninth New Collegiate Dictionary. Springfield, Mass.: Merriam-Webster Inc., 1984 (pp. 9-10)

West Baton Rouge Historical Association. "Louisiana Recipes From West Baton Rouge Historical Association," Port Allen, La. (p.102)

Whittaker, David. Recipe printed in *The Only Texas Cookbook*. Texas Monthly Press, Austin, Tex., now a part of Gulf Publishing Company, Houston, Tex.: Copyright © 1981. Used with permission; all rights reserved (pp. 116)

Index Of Recipes

Books
by
Acadian House
Publishing

The Truth About The Cajuns

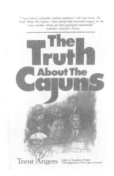

A 120-page hardcover book that describes the French-Acadian, or Cajun, people with the accuracy and dignity to which they are entitled – contrary to the shallow, stereotyping manner in which they have been depicted by many of the news media. This controversial book sets the record straight about the Cajun poeple and their culture. Illustrated with maps and photos. (Author: Trent Angers. ISBN: 0-925417-04-1. Price: $11.95)

Louisiana's French Heritage

A 192-page hardcover book about the French contribution to the colonization of the New World. It describes the settlement of the Acadian Peninsula, the discovery and exploration of the Mississippi River, the development of the first Louisiana colony and the exile of the French-Acadians from Canada. Illustrated with maps and historical drawings. (Author: Truman Stacey. ISBN: 0-925417-02-5. Price: $14.95)

Cajun Country Tour Guide and Festival Guide

A comprehensive guide to 400 tourist attractions and 85 festivals in the 22-parish area of south Louisiana known as "Cajun Country." It is complete with maps locating the sites, hours, phone numbers and fees, an index, as well as feature stories and brilliant color photography. (ISBN: 0-925417-07-6. Price: $5.00)

Dudley LeBlanc: A Biography

A 104-page softcover book about Dudley LeBlanc, the most famous Cajun of all time, and unquestionably one of Louisiana's most unforgettable characters. The political leader of the Cajun people in the 1930s, '40s, '50s and '60s, "Coozan Dud" also invented and promoted HADACOL into the best-selling patent medicine in America in its time. (Author: Trent Angers. ISBN: 0-925417-12-2. Price: $9.95)

Louisiana Festivals Cookbook

A 218-page hardcover book that just may be the most beautiful book on Louisiana cuisine in existence today. It features many of the real classics of Louisiana cooking, as well as nutritional data on the content of each of these recipes. It also features stories about 25 of the state's most fun-filled festivals, plus colorful illustrations which reflect the themes of these festivals. (ISBN: 0-925417-10-6. Price: $21.95)

Cajun Cooking, Part 1...

...contains about 400 of the best Cajun recipes, like Jambalaya, Crawfish Pie, Filé Gumbo, Cochon de Lait, Chicken & Okra Gumbo, Sauce Piquante. Special features include a section on homemade baby foods and drawings of classic south Louisiana scenery. (ISBN: 0-925417-03-3. Price: $12.95)

Cajun Cooking, Part 2...

...picks up where Part 1 left off. It contains such delicious dishes as Shrimp & Crab Bisque, Fresh Vegetable Soup, Seafood-Stuffed Bellpepper, Broiled Seafood Platter, Yam-Pecan Cake. The recipes appear in the same easy-to-follow format as in Part 1, except they're in real large print for arm's-length reading. (ISBN: 0-925417-05-X. Price: $9.95)

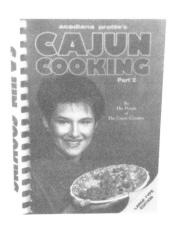

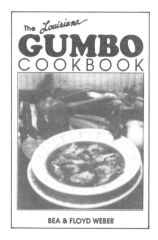

The Louisiana GUMBO Cookbook

A 192-page hardcover book with more than 100 recipes for the Cajun and Creole gumbo dishes that have made south Louisiana food world-famous. Special sections on the history of gumbo and filé, plus instructions for making rice and gumbo stocks. (Authors: Bea & Floyd Weber. ISBN: 0-925417-13-0. Price: $14.95)

Order Form

To order, simply photocopy this Order Form, fill it in, and mail it along with your check or credit card authorization to: Acadian House Publishing, P.O. Box 52247, Lafayette, LA 70505.

Quantity	Item Number	Title / Item Description	Price Per Item	Total Price

Sub-Total	
Sales Tax: 7.5% for LA residents	
Shipping & Handling: $2 first book; $1 each book thereafter	
TOTAL	

☐ Enclosed is my check or money order for $_____

☐ I'd rather charge it. Please charge $ _____ to my ☐ VISA ☐ MC

Acct. # ⬚⬚⬚⬚⬚⬚⬚⬚⬚⬚⬚⬚⬚⬚⬚⬚⬚

_____   _____
Expiration   Signature

* When placing orders for shipment out of the U.S., add 50% to shipping & handling rates.

Ordered by:

_____
Name

_____
Address

_____
City, State, Zip

Ship to

_____
Name

_____
Address

_____
City, State, Zip

Questions? Call (318) 235-8851

Want to learn more about Louisiana's intriguing culture, heritage and history?

Much of what you may want to know can be found in the books published by Acadian House Publishing, including these:

- ◆ *Louisiana's French Heritage*
- ◆ *The Truth About The Cajuns*
- ◆ *Cajun Cooking Cookbooks (A set of 2)*
- ◆ *Cajun Country Tour Guide & Festival Guide*
- ◆ *Louisiana Festivals Cookbook*
- ◆ *Louisiana Gumbo Cookbook*
- ◆ *Dudley LeBlanc: A Biography*

For more information, turn to page 189